# Pup for Beginners

## How to easily raise a puppy to be the darling of your neighbourhood

**Martin André Cessar**

## Disclaimer

This work is protected by copyright. The translation and reproduction of this work or parts of this work are prohibited without the express permission of the author. The implementation of the methods presented in the book is at your own risk.

The publisher and the author can neither assume liability for personal injury, property damage or financial loss nor guarantee the accuracy and timeliness of the information contained herein. Please note that the content of this work is based on the personal opinion of the author and may not be equated with medical help. Please consult your physician about the recommendations presented in this book before you follow them. Neither the author nor the publisher can guarantee that the objectives will be achieved. Furthermore, this book contains links to other websites, for whose content no responsibility is taken. At the time of writing this book, no legal violations of linked websites could be detected.

# Table of Contents

Preface: How to Raise Your Puppy to be a
Happy and Loving Dog Without Stress .................. 5

So You Will Find the PERFECT Puppy for You! ... 8

The Puppy Moves In: How He Feels
Comfortable With You From The Beginning ........ 21

5 Most Common Mistakes and
How to Avoid Them ............................................. 36

The Healthy Development of the Puppy .............. 41

Happy Relationship With Your Puppy:
How to Gain Attachment, Respect and Trust ........ 47

Raising Without Treats ........................................ 55

The 13 Most Important Trainings That Will
Make Your Puppy an Absolute Favorite! ............. 62

Basic Commands -
Teach the First Commands Very Easily ............... 90

Everything You Should Know About
Health, Nutrition & Sleep of the Puppy .............. 105

How Your Puppy Finds True Friends ................. 115

Children & Puppies -
Living Together Peacefully ................................. 124

A Well-Behaved Puppy ....................................... 133

With or Without Dog School .............................. 133

Punishment Without Violence! ........................... 137

Successful Clicker Training With a Puppy ......... 140

Pay Attention to These 6 Things and
Your Puppy Training Will Be 100% Successful . 145

BONUS: 10 Dog Games for Indoors & Outdoors 157

# Preface: How to Raise Your Puppy to be a Happy and Loving Dog Without Stress

A dream comes true: You finally get a puppy! This is a totally beautiful moment when you pick up the dog and offer him a new home with you. Of course, you know that this also brings with it a responsibility. You want to raise the puppy properly to avoid trouble and to make you **feel super comfortable with each other**. There are a lot of things to consider when raising a puppy. To do everything right, you hold the ideal book in your hands.

With this book I will guide you **step by step** through all the important areas of puppy training. With the help of the highly effective advice and tips, you will raise the **perfect puppy**, promote his healthy development, and build an incredibly **happy relationship with him**. Many proud dog owners have done many things wrong. So that you do not repeat this, I will tell you the **5 most common mistakes and how to avoid them**.

Besides the basic commands and the 13 most important trainings you will learn everything you need to know about the nutrition, sleep, and health of your puppy. I am especially happy to show you how to **train** the dog **completely without violence and without treats**. You are even able to save yourself from dog school by simply implementing these lessons that are suitable for everyday life. This way, your puppy will become a lovely, well-behaved dog that everyone loves. So that you two **have a lot of fun,** and he learns something at the same time, I'm giving a great **bonus** in this edition: **10 dog games** for indoors & outdoors.

I think it is a pity when inexperienced dog owners make many mistakes, cause the dog severe suffering, and stress themselves enormously. But life could be so much better for the dog and his owner, if you only consider a few basic things.
It is exactly these important basics that I give you on your way. I am convinced:

- Anyone can **train** their **puppy correctly** with effective and clever methods.

- Mistakes can easily be avoided if you prepare yourself optimally.

- You too can build a beautiful relationship with your puppy and see him grow into a well-behaved dog.

For this reason, it is very important to me that this book gives you tips that will actually give you an enormous advantage.

In the following chapters you will therefore get **exact instructions**, which you can easily follow.

The first step for the right puppy training is to read this book carefully and make some notes. So, when you are ready, get yourself some paper and a pen, then make yourself comfortable in a place where nobody can disturb you.

**Let's get going!**

# So You Will Find the PERFECT Puppy for You!

You have decided: You want to have a puppy. This is a wonderful idea.

But which puppy should it be? How so you make a good choice? What is the secret recipe for finding the perfect puppy? The choice of a puppy is something very personal and varies from person to person. Granted, there is no secret formula, but there are certain factors that can help you choose a suitable puppy that will stand by you for 10 or 15 years. Here are some considerations you should take into account when looking for a puppy.

**Get to know the parents.**

In my opinion this is the best advice to determine the nature of a puppy (i.e. the character the puppy is likely to show when he is grown up). It is very important to know the parents of a puppy before choosing one to make sure that he has grown up in the right conditions. Of course, this is not always possible, because when we talk about rescued dogs or sheltered animals, in most cases we have no information about their past and even less about their parents (we may not even know which breed they belong to).

It is especially interesting to know the mother, because she usually has more influence in the first weeks of the puppy's life. Factors such as social integration, or the dog's independence, depend largely on the relationship with the mother. Maybe you are not interested in puppies that have had an overly protective or overly independent litter mother.

## The puppy should have direct contact with other dogs.

To ensure that the puppy is compatible and sociable, the mother should ideally have given birth to several puppies. In this way, the puppy will have social interaction with other dogs from the very beginning and will learn important manners.

There should be at least two puppies in the litter, so that the puppy can interact with another dog besides the mother. It is also not good if the litter is too big, because it becomes more difficult for the mother to take care of all of them. From 10 puppies on it is considered a large litter. However, it also depends on the experience of the mother (whether it is her first litter or whether she has had several).

**Be clear about what kind and breed you want.**

It seems very obvious, but experience teaches us that many people want a dog. But they don't really know which one, and that's the important thing. You should look for a type of dog that fits your lifestyle.
And to clarify this point, we start from the following premise: There is no such thing as a perfect dog.

Every puppy can become a wonderful companion, if it is socialized and educated in the right way, and every puppy can also become an "evildoer," if things are done wrong. Whatever kind of dog you are looking for, remember that it is up to you to train him to be a good dog.

Whether you want a purebred or a mixed breed is a very personal decision. The main difference is that dogs of certain breeds usually have a more predictable appearance and behavior. You should pay attention to this and see if it matches what you are looking for. Mongrels, however much we try to look for similarities, are always unique (and wonderful) individuals. This fact also means that mixed-breed dogs are generally healthier and have a longer life expectancy (due to less inbreeding).

If you choose a breed, it is an advantage to know it well. What are their main characteristics and features, what are their main difficulties, how active is the dog, what can you expect in the next years in the relationship with this dog.
Be careful, not every person will advise you correctly on this topic. To do everything right, you have to know the breed really well. There are many people and even professionals who base their opinion on stereotypes or preconceived ideas that are far from reality.

It is important to keep this in mind because once you have the puppy at home you will see that he is growing at a pretty dizzying rate, and in just 4 months he will have become a teenage dog with most of the strength, agility and size of an adult dog, but whose mind is still that of a puppy.

## Health

If you attach importance to keeping a healthy dog, then pay attention to the following characteristics:
**Eyes**: Some puppies may have vision problems or be blind. To make sure that this is not the case, it is best to observe the puppy, check that it does not bump into things that are in its way, and see if it moves.

**Hair**: Look clean and neat.

**Ears**: Check if he's deaf. Make small noises with your hands or fingers near his ears to make sure he reacts.

**Movement**: Look at how he moves and make sure that he does not limp.

**Physical**: The puppy should be in a normal condition. He should not be too thin, obese, or have a belly that is too big.

**Respiration**: A healthy puppy should be able to breathe normally without difficulty.

**Hygiene**: Make sure that both the puppy and his siblings have good hygiene.

To be inclusive, I do not want to speak out against sick puppies under any circumstances. Of course, they can give just as much or much more pleasure. Just keep in mind that you will have more work to do and consider absolutely if you want and can take this responsibility.


**5 questions you should ask yourself when you are looking for a puppy.**

If you are still thinking about what kind of dog you would like to have, these questions will help you a lot in your final decision.

1. What lifestyle do I have?
Just now, in the present.

Don't trust the "...but if I have a dog, I will do this and that...".

Most people's schedules are overcrowded, so be realistic and pay attention to the everyday life you lead today. For example, if you work long hours or are a less active person, don't look for a dog that needs a lot of activity, because it might demand a lot from you.

2. In which environment do I live?
Dogs can adapt to almost any environment, but if you live in a very central urban or rural area, it may be easier for you to choose one breed or another.

It can also be important how big your home is, what other creatures (animals and humans, including children) live at home, whether you have your own car, etc...
Also pay attention to how big the dog will become. Do you have enough space for him to move freely, eat, and sleep?

There are breeds that are more suitable for living with children (Boxer, Labrador, Golden), but I think that if we educate the dogs and the children well, any breed is fine to live with them, even more so if the dog comes into the family as a puppy.

We also need to consider whether there are older people living at home. Quiet breeds of small to medium size adapt better to them, although with proper training, any dog can be a good companion for older people.

3. Is this my first dog?
If you are a "newcomer," there are a number of breeds that you should be careful of, as they can be more difficult dogs. This does not mean that you cannot take them, but you should be aware that it will require extra effort if you decide to take them. There is nothing wrong with these dogs. But you have to remember that driving a 90 HP Seat is not the same as driving a 500 HP Ferrari.

4. How much time do I have?
If you don't have much time, it might be best to check whether you really should own a dog.
All dogs need a good amount of time and energy, and when we talk about hunting dogs or shepherd dogs, for example, you need a large portion of both.

5. Why do you want the dog?
It is important to pay attention to this, because we have to choose a breed that fits what we want.

If you want him as a companion for many wonderful years of life, then in principle, any dog can be a great companion.

Maybe you like sports such as cycling or running, in which case you should look for a dog with a high energy level to accompany you on your runs/drives in the country or in the city.

It is not always easy to choose a puppy, and nobody can assure us that the puppy you choose will be great or a care. The best way for you to ensure that your puppy will be an affable and sociable dog for the rest of his life is to take his socialization and education seriously. I already told you that much of a dog's behaviour depends on it.

So be aware of this. Find a trainer, sign him up for puppy classes and work with him.

Another important aspect in choosing the right puppy is the breeder.

**What makes a good breeder?**

A puppy does not have its first learning experiences
when it comes to you. He learns from the day he is
born. This means that when he comes to you, he has
already had eight or twelve weeks of experience at a
particularly formative age. That's why they should be
especially good. To get a dog with whom you can
work well, you should take a good look at the breeder.
If you choose a breeder, it is not important that he
lives nearby. It is better to go far than to support a
breeder who has badly socialized dogs.

During the first phone call you can already ask some
relevant questions. For example, the breeder should be
able to answer you if the birth went without any
problems and if all puppies survived. It can happen
that puppies die at birth or shortly after.
However, the breeder should be able to tell you what
they died of, so that hereditary diseases can be
excluded. You can also ask if the mother takes good
care of the puppies, and if there is enough milk for all
puppies. Also make sure that you like the breeder.

If the first telephone call is positive, a first visit to the
breeder follows. No matter what the breeder tells you,

never get involved with the fact that the puppy will be brought to you or that you will buy him out of a car. Behind such offers there is usually cruel breeding. A serious breeder should have no problem if you come to his home and have a look at his breeding facility. This is the only way to make sure that you do not support cruelty to animals, and that you bring a healthy dog into your home.

When you are at the breeder's home, you should be able to take a close look at the mother and all puppies. Make sure that all the dogs are well fed and look healthy. The environment in which the puppies grow up should be neat and clean. Observe carefully if the puppies seek contact with humans.

It is also important how the mother dog reacts to your visit. She should be calm or at least be reassured by her owner. This speaks for a good relationship to the breeder. The puppies look at this behaviour of their mother. Nevertheless, keep some distance from the puppies in the beginning. It is perfectly ok that the mother dog does not let anybody touch her puppies. You should also take a look at the psychological condition of the puppies. They should be curious and lively. Of course, they should also be in good physical condition. Sticky eyes, nasal discharge, sneezing, coughing, or diarrhea are signs of illness.

During the first visit you should ask some questions:

- When will the puppies be delivered?
  A serious breeder would never hand over his puppies before the eighth week. If the breeder wants to give them to you earlier, this indicates that he does not pay much attention to the well-being of the puppies.

- What have the puppies gotten to know so far?
  At a young age it is especially important that a puppy gets to know everything he will come into contact with later. If the puppies grow up in a house in the forest, this is indeed a great environment for dogs. However, if the puppies do not make regular trips to the city, they will be completely overwhelmed by life in the city. This will cause you, as a future owner, a lot of problems. Make sure that the breeder drives a car with the puppies, gets them used to children, elderly people, other animals and other dogs.

- What do the puppies and the mother dog eat? Make sure that the food contains many important nutrients.

- Are the dogs wormed? A serious breeder only gives away dewormed puppies.

- Are the puppies vaccinated and chipped? This is unavoidable. If a breeder wants to give you an unvaccinated and unchipped puppy, you should consider this.

- Is there a recommendation for a puppy? This does not mean that the breeder should tell you which puppy is the best, but which puppy fits best to you and your needs. Therefore, he should ask you which dog you want and how your daily routine is. A serious breeder does not give his puppies to just anyone. After all, he wants to know that his dogs are doing well.

- What is the delivery procedure? An experienced breeder can give you some valuable tips on how to make the day of departure easier for your dog. We will come to this in the next chapter.

# The Puppy Moves In: How He Feels Comfortable With You From The Beginning

It is the most exciting day in the life of a dog owner. The little sweet puppy is moving in. You have already visited him several times at the breeder and you have chosen the puppy that will enrich your life in the future. He is the sweetest little creature on the planet and you want to roll out the red carpet for him and spoil him from front to back. But that is exactly the problem.

Education is the most important thing in living together with a dog. You must be able to control your dog and show him how to behave properly. Only then can you live together with him in a relaxed way. And education does not only start when your dog is grown up. It starts on the first day. Your puppy must know immediately where to go. But this is where the problem begins. When you pick up your first dog, you are probably a bit overwhelmed at the beginning. There is so much to think about and learn. You will definitely not do everything right. But don't worry, this is absolutely normal.

No one is perfect and no one will always do everything right. When you have your first dog, you have to try a lot of things first. If you make a mistake, that is not bad. The important thing is that you constantly educate yourself and learn more. This is the only way you can improve in the future and become the best owner for your dog.

**Pick up from the breeder**

What should the pick up look like ideally, when you pick up the puppy at the breeder, the car ride, etc.? For you, the arrival of the puppy is connected with a lot of excitement. But for the puppy, it can be scary and sad because he has to leave his mommy and home, as well as become familiar with his new surroundings and people.

Ideally, two of you will travel together, so one of you can drive the car while the other takes care of the puppy and makes him feel safe.

It is very important that you make an appointment with the breeder in advance, so that the breeder does not feed the puppy before. If he has eaten before, he might throw up. Therefore, it is better to pick him up on an empty stomach.

Another very important point: When you arrive at the breeder to pick up the puppy, you should not push him quickly over the checkout belt and rush him away like a carton of milk in the supermarket. Don't take him away directly, but try to gain the puppy's trust at the beginning by consciously playing with treats, for example. Most of the time the puppies are already coming over to you. But it is important that he follows you more or less to the car. Otherwise he will have a negative experience with a strange man/woman coming and packing him into the car. Entice him, activate his nose, and gain his trust. so that he doesn't associate anything negative with you later on.

Once you have the puppy in the car, it should be on the lap of the passenger during the drive and, ideally, you should have a blanket with you that smells like his home. What you can do is, if you visit the puppy regularly, you should leave a blanket with the breeder beforehand so that it can absorb all the smells. When you pick up the puppy, put him on this blanket. Then he will at least have his usual smells with him, which is a relief for him.

An important point is to bring enough kitchen rolls and towels, something to drink, of course, and also treats. It can happen that the puppy might pee in the car because of excitement and then at least you have the correct supplies with you to clean up.
If you have a long car journey, remember to plan enough breaks, because your puppy has to go to the toilet, especially if the puppy has a totally untrained bladder.

Take a harness with you. If you stop somewhere, the puppy can be gone quickly, because he has no bond to you yet. Therefore, you should put on a leash or a harness. Then you have him with you and allow the puppy the breaks, because it is a lot of stress for him.

**Separation from the mother**

I explain the steps you have to take so that neither the puppy nor the mother suffers physically or mentally when they separated.

You should be aware that the mother's milk contains important nutrients for the development of her puppy's immune system. Therefore, you should let him suckle for a while so he can develop. In addition, contact with the mother will help him learn social behavior with other puppies and even with humans. As already mentioned in the previous chapter about the breeder, you should wait at least two months before separating the mother and child. If you do this earlier, you might hinder his development and your pet might even get sick. Pay attention to basic grooming, as dogs at this age can suffer from diseases that can be fatal.

If it is a small dog that has not yet been vaccinated, you should prevent it from leaving your yard so it does not catch diseases.
You should also avoid contact with stray dogs, although it is not a problem if he is with other pets as long as you are sure that they are fully vaccinated. In fact, when he comes into contact with other dogs, he quickly learns some basic behavior. He knows whether he can bark, where he can be, and even whether he can climb on the sofas or not, just by watching others.

## Doing everything right from the start

The pressure to do everything right is present in everyone. You should ignore this pressure from the beginning, because you will not be able to do it anyway. So, don't stress yourself if you realize that you have made a mistake. Nevertheless, it is important that you educate yourself as well as possible. The right education should play a role in the dog's everyday life from the beginning, from the first second on. If your puppy is not supposed to be on the couch, he should not be allowed to do so in the first days either. The rules must be established immediately. Nevertheless, it is okay that you are a little lenient in the first few days. Always remember that you have separated your puppy from his family and his breeder. This is a difficult step for him, and you have to be there for him. He may therefore need a lot of love and attention.

In the first few days, staying alone plays absolutely no role. Your puppy should also not spend the first night alone. He needs the feeling that someone else is there for him. You see, it's important that you find a happy medium. A bit of indulgence is okay in the first few days, but that doesn't mean that you should let your puppy get away with everything. The foundation for a good upbringing is laid early.


**A safe home for the puppy**

When you have chosen a good breeder, you make sure that your new dog has the best start in life. Before he moves in with you, you should make your apartment puppy proof. A puppy is a very excited being that wants to explore everything. Sometimes he comes up with ideas that you wouldn't have thought of in your dreams. That's why you should clear all possible danger spots before you move him in.

 It is especially important that you keep all doors and windows closed. Otherwise your puppy will surely take the opportunity to break out.
Everything that is fragile should be kept in a cupboard. Your dog must not have the opportunity to break anything, because he could injure himself on the broken pieces.

You should also find out which of your house plants are poisonous to dogs. These must either be placed high up or banned from the house altogether. To determine the type of plant, there are several apps; experts in garden centers can also help you.

In everyday life you have to make sure that the doors of dishwashers, refrigerators, stoves, washing machines, and dryers are always closed. You should hide all electrical cables behind furniture or cable protectors.

Remember that everything that is on open shelves below could be destroyed by your dog. It is better to put unimportant things there. Shoes are very popular with puppies and are often destroyed, so a shoe cupboard is a good idea. This way, your puppy has no chance of stealing your shoes.

Long tablecloths or curtains should be shortened so that your dog cannot get at them.

Plastic shopping bags can become a danger for your dog. He could suffocate or choke himself while playing with them; you should always put them away.

Fire is, of course, always a danger for an excited puppy, so fireplaces should be adequately secured.

If you keep your tables and work surfaces clean and free of food debris, your dog will not be tempted to jump up there. Any leftover food that could harm your dog must be disposed of immediately. Also make sure that your dog does not have the opportunity to tip over and clean out your garbage.

Puppies sometimes get the idea to jump onto the toilet or drink from it; be sure to always close the lid.

All stairs must be blocked with a baby gate to prevent your puppy from falling down them.

## Initial equipment

Beds and baskets

A bed is part of the basic equipment for puppies. They must have their own place in the house where they can relax. To make them comfortable, it is best to provide them with a dog bed or a dog basket, which are available in different shapes and sizes. It is up to you to decide which one you choose. Make sure that the space for your dog is large enough. Your dog should be able to stretch out in it. The baskets should have a removable cushion that can be washed.

Water bowl

Your puppy needs bowls for dog food and water. The bowls should have a stable base so that the dog cannot easily tip it over. Usually the bowl is wider at the bottom than at the top and is made of plastic, stainless steel or ceramic.

## Collars and harnesses

Collars and harnesses should not be missing in the basic equipment for puppies. There is an infinite number of models and shapes. When choosing a dog collar, it is very important that it is the right size and adjustable in width. Please check the fit of the collar on the puppy every week. For dogs with long or thick hair I recommend a thick and braided collar that does not get tangled easily. Collars with plastic fasteners are only suitable for small or tame dogs, because they break when pulled strongly.

## Leash

The leash should correspond to the size of the dog and be comfortable to hold in the hand. Simple nylon or leather leashes are sufficient for small dogs. These should be strong enough not to tear when the dog is on the leash and should also be long enough to allow freedom of movement. Automatic or extendable dog leashes, such as Flexi leashes, are also very good options. On the other hand, dogs of large and medium breeds need robust leashes with an adjustable length of at least two meters.

## For puppy care

Usually a brush, comb and dog shampoo are sufficient. The hair type of the dog determines everything else. For dogs with long hair, which tends to get tangled up, we recommend detangling sprays. However, these are not suitable for greasy hair. You may also consider using something for ear cleaning and nail clippers.

## Dog tag

The identification of the dog is crucial for its safety. One of the first things you should do is to order a dog tag with his name, your phone number and your name, unless the breeder has already chipped him. So, if your puppy disappears during a walk, the person who finds him can help you get him back.

## Toys

Playing helps the dog to maintain its mental balance and strengthen the relationship with its owner. Most of these accessories for dogs are made of vinyl or solid rubber. Care should be taken with small dog toys, as they can get stuck in the dog's throat and in the worst case, can lead to suffocation. This can also happen with throwing games and with sticks. Discs or frisbees are completely harmless.

## Clicker

The Clicker is a practical tool for dog training. It is a small device. With it you can make a clicking sound when you press it. It is designed to attract the dog's attention and make him/her carry out the commands you give him/her at the moment you click.

## Dog food

Before you buy a large amount of dog food, you should talk to both the dog breeder and your veterinarian. Choosing a high quality food is an important factor for the health of your dog, and it is worth consulting professionals before making a decision.

## How does a puppy learn best?

You have now given your puppy the best start in life by choosing a good breeder and providing a safe home. This makes the upbringing much easier for you. But before you start, you should be aware of how your puppy learns best. Puppies are still very young, insecure, and curious dogs. They learn about the world by imitating their role models. In the beginning, this is the mother. Later the owner is the role model in the best case. You have to be a good role model. Be relaxed and go through different situations with confidence. Your dog will copy this behaviour from you and will orient itself to you. Always remember that your puppy will watch you every second of the day, and will judge you by your behavior. He will remember how you behave in certain situations. He will observe whether you are friendly or aggressive towards other dogs and people, and will copy this from you.

A dog quickly divides its life into rituals. At mealtime he will stare at you hungrily. If you always take his food out of the fridge, he will jump up every time you open the fridge, because he connects the fridge with his food.

He makes such connections very quickly, so make sure your dog makes mainly positive and not negative connections. Only in this way can he go through life with an open mind. These connections are created through classical conditioning. If he is always stroked as soon as he looks at you, he will show this behaviour every time he wants to be stroked.

You use this conditioning to help you train your dog to behave in the desired way. This is the way in which your dog learns particularly well. As soon as he shows a behavior that you like, you reward him. This positive reinforcement makes your dog especially motivated to participate in the training. And your bond is strengthened.

The situation is different if you use inappropriate and outdated training methods based on fear, intimidation, or even pain. You will lose your dog's confidence and he will not want to train. You will not be able to build a close relationship with your dog.That doesn't mean that you can't be strict and tell your puppy if you don't like something. But this must be done without fear and pain.

You can use light measures to show your dog that something does not suit you.

This includes:

- Ignore

- Game termination

- abort signal

- Slight impact in the neck area (be especially careful here. The dog should not be injured,

but only notice that you do not like this
behavior).

The education of your puppy should mainly be based
on positive reinforcement. Punishments are only a
small part of the upbringing and should be used
selectively. Arbitrary punishments give your dog the
feeling that he cannot judge you, and do not lead to
learning success.

# 5 Most Common Mistakes and How to Avoid Them

## 1. Severe overload

The first mistake is that the puppies are totally overwhelmed in the first two or three days. The dog owners are so happy that they now have the puppy at home, that they would love to share their happiness with everyone they know. This means that the puppy is shown to the aunts, uncles, grandmas, grandpas, and the whole neighbourhood. Or he is brought directly to the first park and the whole family wants to walk the dog. In the first few days the dog will be so overwhelmed with impressions that it will feel beaten to death.

You can easily avoid this by taking a lot of rest in the first two or three days. Of course, be happy that you have your puppy at home now, but give him the opportunity to get used to the new environment slowly and calmly. Make sure that you gradually introduce him to new stimuli without overtaxing him.

## 2. Insufficient socialization of the puppy

It is not enough to take your new dog to a dog school or to a puppy play group. That alone is not socialization. Socialization is experiencing many new and unknown situations with your dog. You will find yourself calmly and quietly next to him so that he can feel safe during these experiences; so your puppy will realize: "This is not a bad thing, this does not hurt me, and nothing bad happens to me here".

Go into a train station; there are strange noises, there are people with suitcases, honking trains, and business people on the phone.

Go to a supermarket with the puppy. Stay very relaxed so that the dog can see on you that everything is fine.

You do the same at a kindergarten or school. Just stand outside by the fence when the kids are outside. He must simply feel that there is no danger from the many noisy children.  This is a socialization of the puppy.


## 3. Too high expectations of the puppy

First time owners often think, "He can do nothing at all, he is not house-trained, he does not sit, does not even react to his name." The puppy has perhaps only been there two days and just in the eighth or ninth week of life. That cannot work. Of course, the dog is not able to do many things by himself. Maybe he has been socialized a little bit by the breeder and that's it. That means, all these things that you want from the dog, you must teach him over time.

Time is the right keyword. It just takes a certain amount of time until he is out of the rough. But already in the 8th, 16th or 20th week of life, to think that the dog must be able to do everything, is wrong. If he can't do that, you panic. This is a completely exaggerated expectation to the dog. Take at least one year to train the dog really well. Then you will have really good results.

## 4. Let the puppy go ahead

For a dog, being in front means taking responsibility.
That means for him, you send him into the world, into
life, and tell the puppy, who has no life experience at
all, "You go ahead, be responsible for us up there."
Puppies are naturally overburdened with this. The
worst thing is what happens in the head of the dogs
and that they feel left alone by their master/mistress.
The dog may lose confidence in you and will later
manage all other situations for itself. Because to be
ahead once means to be the boss. This is the role he
wants to carry all the time. But you are the one who is
in front, not the puppy.


## 5. No knowledge about dogs and their learning behavior

This is also a problem especially for first-time owners
who have considered getting a dog. They did not deal
with the matter at all before, but simply got a dog and
think that it will become somehow. Then at the
beginning, a lot of things go wrong, in the first days
or maybe the first week until you maybe go to a dog

trainer. He will show you how a dog learns, because it is completely different from how we humans learn. We humans can reflect behavior. This means that if a child has done something wrong, you can explain to him afterwards that he has done something wrong. But if a dog, let's say, did not come back, although you called him, and only comes back sometime later. If you would punish him for not coming, he would not learn anything. On the contrary, it only learns that coming back is punished.

That you bought this book is already an important step to acquiring the necessary knowledge about dogs. You learn here how to raise your puppy correctly. I hope you can avoid the mistakes described here. You and your dog will have it so much easier.

# The Healthy Development of the Puppy

At a young age, living beings develop particularly rapidly. Each developmental phase must be used optimally. Therefore, you should be aware of when your dog is in which phase.

### The first time at the breeder

In the first and second week of your puppy's life, you are not yet present in his life. Nevertheless, he already has valuable experiences. This time is called the *neonatal phase*. The puppy learns to feel body heat and to move his head easily. This is essential for him to survive. Because only in this way will he be able to find his way back to his mother and milk. The sense of smell and the sense of taste are already present, so the puppy can find the teat. It explores its environment only with these two senses. During this time the puppy does not do much more than cuddling with his siblings and sucking at the mother's teat. From the third week of life, the puppy is able to hear and see. Therefore, he now has many new experiences. He reacts to sounds and gets to know his environment in a completely new way. During this time, a puppy starts to leave the nest and start its own exploratory tours. At this time it is even possible to begin house training. However, this is the breeder's task at this age. If from the third week on they only do their business in the garden or in boxes with natural ground, you as the owner will have it easier with house training later on.

**The socialization phase**

In the fourth week of your puppy's life, the socialization phase begins. This usually has already begun from the 21st day of life. It goes then up to the 12th or 1th week of life. You as the future owner will probably adopt your dog in exactly this phase. The breeder and you will share the time. Your dog must now gain a lot of experience because in this time, the basis for his later behavior is set. He must now get to know everything that he will encounter later in life. This includes cars, streets, other dogs, people, children, bikes, skateboards, and much more. But you should also think about the little things. In the socialization phase, your dog should already get his first bath so that he gets used to it. He has to get to know vacuum cleaners, brooms, elevators, TVs, different floor coverings, dishwashers, lawnmowers and many other things.

Also get him used to you touching his paws, looking into his mouth and ears and turning him on his side. Once he gets used to this, visits to the vet will be much more relaxed in the future. You have to show your puppy a lot during this time. At the same time, you should also make sure that he gets enough sleep because for him these are all strong stimuli that he has to process first. If you don't allow him to rest, he will be so stressed at some point that he will negatively link the new stimuli.

**Puberty**

Not only the human children, but also the puppies reach puberty. Just like with our children, it is a stressful time when your dog will question everything. You have to enforce every rule again. The memory does not count anymore. Everything else is much more interesting. Your dog starts to defend his territory and to show other adult behaviors. He puts his childhood aside and dares to make the leap to an adult dog. It may be that you despair of your dog. Many dogs are extremely exhausting during this time.

Nevertheless, it is completely wrong to shout at the dog. Because your dog does not do all this to annoy you. He does it because he himself is insecure and changes a lot in his body. He is looking for his place in life and needs your help. If you offer it to him, your bond can strengthen during this time. So instead of despairing of your dog, you have to spend a lot of time with him. Puberty occurs with every dog at different times. usually between the 7th and 12th months of life.

Train diligently with your dog so that he remembers his previous training and can spend a lot of time with you. Through the rules you set him during puberty, you help him to find his place. Therefore, consistency is very important. Work with a lot of motivational aids so that your dog enjoys training with you. If you think that you are overstrained with your dog during puberty, you can turn to a good dog school.

## The second puberty

Yeah, you read it right. It is not yet done with the first phase of puberty. You are happy that you have your dog under control again to some extent, but then the second phase of puberty begins. In this time, your dog becomes sexually mature. This phase begins at six or twelve months and ends at about 1.5 or 2 years. Male dogs now begin to lift their legs when they pee and bitches become into heat for the first time. Good behavior with your dog in this phase is hard to find. Again, the dog tests his limits. You must be firm with your education. If you were not consistent, this will become apparent now. Make sure that you continue to set clear boundaries for your dog. Some dogs develop various fears during this time because puberty is a very sensitive time. Therefore, be consistent but not harsh. A loving hand is exactly what your dog needs during this time.

It is also possible that your dog suddenly reacts aggressively to other dogs of the same species. Therefore, be especially careful. But don't worry, this time will also pass. If you have survived all puberty phases and have been consistent, you will finally receive your reward: a well-behaved and loving dog who has a good bond with you.

# Happy Relationship With Your Puppy: How to Gain Attachment, Respect and Trust

**This is how you become the "pack boss".**

Do I have to be the pack leader for my dog? This question is asked by almost every new dog owner. You hear from many sides that you have to establish yourself as a pack leader or pack manager. From other sides one hears again the exact opposite. The term "pack leader" is outdated.

Basically it doesn't matter what you want to call yourself. You can call yourself mom, pack leader, or best friend. The important thing is that your dog looks up to you. There is a hierarchy in your relationship. Because dogs are able to consider a human as a full partner. This hierarchy will develop automatically.

47

You should make sure that your dog is subordinate to you, because otherwise he might start to reprimand you, be aggressive towards others (to protect you), or bark at everyone at the front door. You will not be able to eliminate these negative behaviors if you are not the clear leader in your relationship.

Of course this does not mean that you have to suppress your puppy. On the contrary. Dogs see a good leader when they have a calm, loving, and sovereign person in front of them.
Immediately forget all old-fashioned educational methods. These include:

- Canvas print

- Alpha Litter

- Beating

- Screaming

- Choke collars

- Spiked collars

- Pushing dog to the ground

- Throwing objects at the dog

You should do without these things, because they only lead to your dog not trusting you and being afraid of you. This is not a good basis for a relationship. You can establish yourself much better as a pack leader through other things.

In many ways, dogs are very similar to humans. When you think about how to become a good leader for your dog, you only have to think about what you want from a good leader.

You probably imagine a good boss as intelligent, sovereign, fair, loving, strong and considerate.

It is definitely helpful if you are physically superior to your dog. But this is not the only point that makes you a good leader. Your dog must feel that you take the lead in dangerous situations. Show him this through various little things in everyday life.

If a strange dog comes towards you, you greet it first. Then your dog may approach him. In this way your dog notices that you are evaluating the situation.

When the doorbell rings, you are the one who judges whether the situation is dangerous or not. Your dog stays behind until you have decided that everything is okay. When you come home, your dog first goes to the safe house, then you follow. All these and many more little things in everyday life show your dog that you make the decisions and judge situations.

At some point he will ask you for your opinion. If you meet a dog that barks, your dog will give you a questioning look. What you say at that moment is law for your dog. If you say that you give the dog a wide berth, your dog will follow. If you say you are going in the opposite direction, he will follow you as well. If you pass a barking dog, you should make sure that you walk between the foreign dog and your dog. By doing this, you show your dog that you are protecting him. If a strange dog comes storming towards your dog with full force, you stand in between. This gives your dog the security that you are always there for him. All these little things are important to show your dog that he can trust you. You should never force him into situations where he feels uncomfortable. Slowly introduce him to new things and make them fun. Do not try to persuade him. Instead, let him decide for himself when he wants to give the situation a second chance. That way he will realize that you respect him and understand him.

It is equally important that you respond to his body language. If he growls, you should never punish him for it. Otherwise the puppy will think you don't understand him. To be a good leader, you must react to your dog. If he shows fear, be there for him and protect him. Here it is important to find a good balance. Your dog cannot always determine what happens. In situations of fear you must of course be considerate. However, if your dog howls because he wants to be petted, you should never pet him. Otherwise he will learn that you always do what he wants. As soon as he is relaxed and calm, you can pet him.

If you have taught your dog the command "give paw,"he will occasionally hold out his paw to you and say: "Now is the time for food." If you give him something now, he will learn that he determines when it is time for food. Instead, there is only food when he is quiet, you give the command, and he gives you his paw.
All these things you have to pay attention to at any time of the day, because your dog watches your

reactions around the clock. However, it is also understandable that you make mistakes in the beginning. This is not too bad if you learn from your mistakes.

## The right communication with the dog

The be-all and end-all of a good relationship is communication. This applies to us humans and also to dogs. Your dog must understand you and you must understand him. Only in this way can a relationship of trust develop. Pay attention to small signals of your dog.

The wagging tail, for example, is not always a sign of joy. It just means that your dog is excited. You need to pay attention to the rest of his body language to know if your dog is happy or frightened.

If the tail is down and only slightly wagging, this often shows fear. As soon as your dog pinches his tail, this is a sign of severe discomfort. Your dog may have an illness, pain or fear.

By his posture, you can easily see the emotional state of your dog. When his body is relaxed, your dog is relaxed. As soon as your dog's whole body moves back and forth in extension of his tail, he is happy. If your dog's body is tense, he is afraid or aggressive. If he adopts this body posture and at the same time fixes the other dog or person with his eyes, this is a clear threat that becomes even clearer with a growl.

Growling is another way to communicate. It is very important, because with a growl your dog says that he doesn't want something right now. And he should be allowed to do that. However, if your dog growls at you, you have to do something about it. But only with positive reinforcement because your dog does not growl at you to annoy you. He does this because he is fearful. You can only fight these fears with positive reinforcement.

Another kind of communication are the appeasement signals. These may include yawning, turning his head away, slow movements, licking his nose, sniffing the floor, urinating or scratching. You should praise your dog for this, as it avoids conflicts.

Building a good relationship with your puppy from the beginning is important for your whole relationship. Use the advice in this chapter to gain your dog's trust and respect, and to create a strong bond.

Rewards can be one way to do this. How to reward your four-legged friend properly, you will learn in the next chapter.

# Raising Without Treats

### The right reward

Before you start your dog's education, you should be aware that there are different ways of rewarding, and these must be used in different situations.

Food is the most popular reward for many dogs. Especially great treats are only given for especially great behavior.

However, there are many more ways to reward your dog. Never forget verbal praise by telling your dog that he has done something great. Even stroking can be praise. However, not all dogs like that. Always pay attention to the body language.

You might also reward your dog by giving him a great toy or doing a short tug-of-war with him. Running together can also be a reward for the dog. A very popular reward is retrieving. The dog can live out his passion and chase after something. This type of reward is especially suitable for hunting dogs.

Taking your dog to a wide open space, can also be a reward, especially if you are in your dog's favorite meadow. In this case, unleashing will make your dog much happier than any treat.

You must therefore choose the right reward for your dog very carefully. Food is not always the best. Sometimes a game or other reward is much better. A good mix of everything is optimal.

Remember that an overdose of treats can lead to improper nutrition which, if not carefully controlled, can lead to obesity and negatively affect your dog's life. It can also lead to unwanted behavior such as begging.

Are treats always bad?

There are often two opposing opinions on this question. Some forbid treats completely, others are so generous they give the dog a snack on every occasion. As so often, I favor a happy medium.

Food as a treat, is a so-called primary booster for the dog. That means you can reward the dog with it, but you just have to do it right. So, it is not a problem at all if the dog gets a treat from you. Here it also depends a bit on the age of the dog. Especially with puppies who just don't understand yet and don't know what to do, you can work with food. You can get reliable behavior relatively quickly and get the dog moving.

You can also teach the classics like "Sit" or "Space" more quickly than if you do it without treats. Finally, you should ask yourself if you can manage to control your dog completely without treats. If that is possible and you can just ask for it: "Hey, we both walk past other dogs together without treats" or you give another command and it works well, then the social structure is right. In this case there is no reason why you should not reward your dog with a treat every now and then.

Just try to avoid both extremes. Often it is a healthy middle course, which then leads to very good results, especially in the area of young dogs. If you work with puppies or young dogs with treats in the beginning, you often forget to remove the treats and that is a problem. In general, social communication with the dog should always be in the foreground.

For example, you can pet, praise or click: there are many ways to motivate a dog. If you approach your dog training with a lot of praise, you don't necessarily have to resort to treats to be successful. Fortunately, the many alternatives to  snacks show that there is another way.

## Praise and caress

A certain word like "good" or "beautiful" should accompany the training with your faithful friend from the beginning. Speak it out loud, friendly and motivating, to show him that you have noticed and appreciate the good behavior. If you caress your dog lovingly while praising him with words, the positive effect will be even stronger. Many dogs like to be petted on the head - try out which parts your dog likes best and start to praise your dog extensively.

## Play and run

Every animal is different so the praise methods will also differ. If he has a playful playmate at home, he will enjoy playing. After a few training sessions or a walk, during which your young four-legged friend behaved fantastically, it is time to play. It is important that the animal can enjoy the time with its owner according to its taste.

## Clicker Training

Have you heard about it? Clicker training also offers a popular way to educate, motivate, and praise a four-legged friend without treats. Learning the basics may take a little time and patience, but many dog owners still appreciate clicker training as an easy and successful way to train a dog.

Educating with the clicker is different from other training methods because it requires only a few minutes of training. I will go into more detail in a later chapter.

**Your reward list**

If you can't think of any rewards right away when you need them, it's worth preparing a reward list. Write down what can be a reward for your dog. Sure, treats are one possibility. Alternatives are for example toys, common interaction, and the things I just described. All of these could be a reward. But it can also vary depending on the situation.

If you have a dog that feels uncomfortable with the leash because the other dog is too close to him and then he can't get away properly, then it can be a reward for this dog in this situation to increase the distance from the other dog. It can be that the reward is that the dog is allowed to go sniffing for a short time. It may be that the reward is that you run together briefly. You can be really creative.

Everything that makes your dog feel comfortable in that moment is a reward. That means it does not always have to be food. Make a list and think about in which moments you use rewards and in which moments these things are especially exciting and important for your dog. Then it will not be difficult for you to reward in different ways, and you will not get question marks in your head when someone tells you "Just reward without treats".

Of course, you don't have to banish treats completely from the puppy's education. It's best to present them to your four-legged friend as something special and use them only rarely, for example when you're practicing a particularly difficult trick with him. Just like you give gummy bears to a child from time to time without putting a huge portion in the school bag every day.

# The 13 Most Important Trainings That Will Make Your Puppy an Absolute Favorite!

If you adopt an older dog that has already had an owner, this dog usually already knows a thing or two and usually has an acceptable behavior. In this case you usually don't have to train that much anymore. Of course, this depends a lot on the dog. Often you have problems with an older dog with bad previous experiences, so you have to train more again. How much effort your dog brings, does not depend on age, but on character and socialization.

Many things that are normal for most older dogs, a puppy has to learn first. For example, that the dog knows its name. A puppy has to learn a lot until he is well-behaved.

**House-trained without stress**

The topic house-training is the first thing a dog has to learn because nobody wants to keep his dog's business in the house longer than necessary.

There are old-fashioned methods of education where it was said that you should press your dog's nose into his legacies when he has done them in the house. This does not achieve anything for a dog, because he does not understand what you want from him.
When it comes to house-training, punishment makes no sense. You should only work with positive reinforcement. Your dog learns very quickly that he has to do his business outside if it is natural for him to do so. It helps if the puppy has always been outside with the breeder to relieve himself. As soon as he is with you, you must watch him closely.

Pay attention to when your dog needs to relieve himself and take him outside at exactly these times. Usually he has to do his business after waking up, after eating, after playing, and before sleeping. Whenever your dog gets nervous, turns in circles or even whines, he has to go to the "toilet". In this case you should take him outside immediately. If he does his business there, praise him for it.

In the first days and weeks you have to take good care of your dog and, if possible, take him outside whenever he has to pee. Then the house-training will soon be quite normal. Accidents will happen. You should simply ignore them. Punishment is useless, so make your dog's accidents go away and don't talk to your dog about them. Next time you should simply take better care to get your dog out in time.

But what can you do if your dog has relieved himself in your apartment? All dogs have relatively regular peeing places. They like to relieve themselves where it already smells of their own urine. So, if your dog has peed on the carpet, it will quickly become a popular place to pee. To prevent this, you must completely remove the urine smell from the carpet as soon as possible.

For this you can of course give the carpet to a professional cleaner. A professional carpet cleaning will remove the stain very thoroughly and you will have no work to do with it. The urine smell will be completely gone and the carpet will be good as new.

However, as long as your dog is not yet house trained, you should be aware that another accident could happen at any time. If you call a professional cleaning company after every pee incident, it can cost you a lot of money.

For small carpets you can of course choose the easier option and replace the carpet. However, you should only do this when your dog is completely housebroken. Otherwise you may have to buy five new carpets. If the rugs are only small, you should remove them before the puppy moves in. As long as your puppy is not yet house-trained, carpets are a tempting place to pee. If they're not lying around the apartment in the first place, you won't have a problem.

Now, if an accident has happened and you want to quickly cover up the smell, you have to use strong cleaning products. The more chemical the carpet smells, the better. because your dog will most likely not relieve himself there. Of course, you must make sure that these cleaning products do not damage your carpet. Some cleaning products can also cause health problems. Remember that your puppy often walks around with his nose on the floor.

The best remedy for dog urine in the carpet is vinegar. You can drip it on the stain and let it work. After a short time, you can easily remove the urine. To remove the stench completely, you should add some baking soda. This will remove the smell so effectively that your puppy will most likely not be tempted to relieve himself there again.

**The dog learns his name**

Another training step that you should start from the first day is learning the name. Your dog needs to know what his name is so that he understands when you call him. For a start, you train this in a distraction-free environment. The best place to do this is at home, in a room that the dog already knows. It should be quiet in the room. If your dog is not looking at you, say your dog's name. As soon as he looks at you, reward him. Make sure that your dog is not distracted, but only looks around when you say the name. As a reward, you can use food, toys, games and petting. You should choose a mixture of all of these, because your dog should not associate his name with a particular reward, but with himself. He should know that he is meant and must react so that something exciting happens.

This training does not involve punishment either. This would only lead to t your puppy not reacting so well to his name, because he would not associate it with something exclusively positive anymore.

While the training is going on, you have to take care that the dog is not constantly called by its name and then nothing happens. This would ruin the whole training. The name should only be mentioned if a reward follows. But remember, even if your dog knows his name, he should not be called by it all the time.

After all, we humans wouldn't like it either if someone called us by our name constantly and then just looked at us with a grin or ignored us. At some point, we would no longer react to it, because we would not want to. And the same goes for the dog. He should be called only by his name if something happens. This does not always have to be a treat. The name can be followed by a command, a game, petting, leashing, or even a toy.

The only important thing is that you also want something from your dog when you call him. If children live in the household, they absolutely must learn this.

**Weaning off jumping - it's that easy**

Jumping is a completely unpopular phenomenon. Many people find it cute when they are jumped on by a small dog. But some people do not like it. And that is completely understandable. Maybe just because they wear good pants that should not be ruined. If your dog jumps on everyone in an uncontrolled manner, you will have problems. Therefore, you need to be able to control this behavior of your dog. Basically, the jumping is not bad. A puppy does this with an adult dog and licks his lips. By doing this the puppy shows his submissiveness and begs for food. The adult dog then chokes up food and gives it to the puppy. It is a submissive gesture that does not necessarily have to be stopped. This behavior is mostly accepted by adult dogs.

However, people are often more sensitive when they are jumped on by a dog. Finally, there are also people who are afraid of dogs. Children and older people can even be knocked over by a large dog. This can become a real problem.

The longer the dog is allowed to jump, the more it will internalize this behavior. That's why you have to work on it already in puppyhood. As soon as he jumps at you, you turn around wordlessly and ignore him. You do not say a word. As soon as he calms down, he will get a reward. If you do this exercise with your puppy right from the start, he will give up jumping very quickly. However, if you wait until the behavior becomes ritualized, it will be very difficult to train an adult dog.

**Do not bite anyone (really effective!)**

The bite inhibition is the most important thing for dogs to live together with other creatures. A puppy that is born bites unrestrained; he does not know that he can hurt others with it.
It is the same with human children. They beat and kick without inhibition and without malicious intent. Other people tell them that it hurts and that they should be more careful. Only through this do we

humans develop the inhibition against hitting others with full force.

That's how it works with dogs, too. If a puppy bites another puppy and the latter is whimpering in pain, the puppy lets go and realizes that this was not good. However, the bite inhibition that occurs in dogs is different from that of humans because dogs have a clearly thicker skin and additionally fur. Therefore, the biting does not hurt them so fast. Your puppy must learn that he must also be careful with humans.

As long as your puppy is still so young, a bite usually doesn't hurt that much, but he grows up fast. And suddenly a bite is no longer harmless, but can cause real injuries. Therefore, you have to teach your puppy the bite inhibition very early.

This is not difficult at all. You do it similar to the way the dogs do it among themselves. If you play with your puppy and he bites you, you stop the game immediately and ignore your dog for a few seconds. He must realize that he made a mistake. When he has calmed down again, you continue playing. If you are absolutely consistent a few times here, your puppy will quickly understand that he has to be careful.

If you have a puppy that doesn't let go when the game is stopped but continues to bite, you can make a snap grip. You put your hand over the snout of the dog. Of course, you should not hurt him. The hand can be very loose. This is only a sign to your puppy that he should refrain from this behavior.

**Prevent barking**

Barking is a very unpopular habit of dogs. But it is also a method of communication. You should not completely stop your dog from barking, because your dog makes itself understood by barking. However, your dog should not bark at everything and everyone. For this you need good socialization. If your dog is overwhelmed by everything, he often has the urge to bark. A dog that goes through life with confidence rarely barks.

There is no training plan to stop your dog's barking. This is because there are many reasons for barking. If your dog barks out of fear, you can only remove him from the situation and slowly get him used to the scary situation.

Some dogs bark when left alone. Others bark when they want something from their owner. In order to have a dog that barks as little as possible, you need to socialize it optimally and train it well. In this case your dog will rarely see a reason to bark.

You should start at a very young age to make it clear to your puppy that he will not get any reward for barking. If your puppy barks because he wants his toy, because he is bored, hungry or impatient, he should not get exactly what he wants. The toy he wants is placed high up in the cupboard when he starts barking. Only when he has been quiet for a while is he allowed to have the toy. Let a lot of time pass.

As soon as a puppy has the experience only once that barking leads to success, he will try it regularly. Therefore, make sure that your dog's barking never leads to success. If you have him in your arm and he barks because he wants to get down on the ground, keep him in your arm until he stops barking.

**Train begging (if desired)**

Begging is a vital behavior for all dogs. If a puppy wants to survive, it must assert itself and push itself to the teat. A dog that leans back and waits for his food to come to him will not survive for long.

In living together with humans, however, begging is not so important for the dog, because its owner makes sure that the dog is provided for. Therefore, many people cannot stand begging. Whether you want to stop your puppy from begging is up to you. Only very few dogs do not beg at all. If you want your dog not to sit at the table expectantly, you have to make sure that he doesn't succeed once, neither with you nor with anyone else.

And that is the difficulty; other people usually do not stick to the training plan as consistently. They are usually not aware of how much work dog training is. So, if it is really important to you that your dog does not beg at all, you must make it clear to everyone with whom you have dinner how important it is to you that your puppy does not get any food at the table. It is clear that you can only stop your dog from begging if he never gets anything from the table.

Although this training task is so easy, most people find it incredibly difficult because our four-legged friends already know which buttons to push on people.

A sweet look, a light nudge with the snout or paw, and a soft whimper is almost always effective. However, if all this does not work, the dog will fall into a kind of depression. Depressed, he puts his head on his paws. He looks sad and as if he has given up. However, as soon as a hand moves towards the ground, the dog stands upright again. If you want to stop your dog from begging, you have to be strong here. But all other people must remain strong as well.

Now the question arises whether you have to wean your dog off begging at all. Everyone must decide that for himself. Basically, begging is not bad. However, it can be annoying when you go to a restaurant with your dog. Some dogs beg very offensively, maybe even loudly and beg also at the tables of strangers. In this case, the dog is not really suitable for a restaurant. However, you can also teach your dog appropriate begging behavior. There is food when your dog sits sweetly and nicely beside the table and looks at you. But as soon as he whines, barks or uses his snout or paw, there is nothing. This does not make your dog stop begging, but it does direct him in a pleasant direction. So, you can go with your dog relaxed to restaurants. Because nobody will complain about a sweet look.

However, if you are annoyed that your dog lies beside the table and begs you every day, you have to make him stop begging.

**Getting used to the leash**

The leash is unnatural for any dog. However, it is absolutely essential in the relationship between man and dog. This is not because we want to restrict our dog. We want to protect him. There are simply too many dangers lurking on the streets of cities for us to let a small, high-spirited puppy run free. If you have trained your dog perfectly, you might be able to let him run free almost all the time. But when you have just picked up your puppy, leashes are mandatory because you do not know him well enough to judge his behavior. He could run away and run into the street.

As important as the leash is, it is unusual for the puppy. You have to get him used to it slowly. For this you start with the collar. You put this around your dog's neck and let him walk around the house a little with it. At some point you take it off again. The dog has learned that the collar is not a limitation and not a real problem.

At some point you can attach a leash to the collar and let your dog run around with it for a while. He should just get used to it.
 The first walks should be short and in quiet places.

However, getting used to the leash has nothing to do with relaxed walking on the leash. At first your puppy will tend to pull on the lead. You should be careful not to pull back.

Above all, you should make sure from the beginning that your puppy is not successful with his pulling on the leash. As soon as he pulls in one direction, you stop or go in the other direction. When the leash is relaxed again, your puppy can go to the object of his desire. The best way to train your puppy for successful and targeted leash control is to change direction each time the leash is tightened. Your dog will eventually become so confused that he will orientate himself towards you and look at you from time to time. You should definitely reward this. Either with a word of praise or even a treat. In between you should also give your puppy the opportunity to work off his energy. Afterwards he can concentrate much better on you and the training.

Getting used to the leash is usually very quick. On the other hand, line training requires much more patience.

**Leave alone**

No puppy can be left alone by nature. This is because dogs normally spend every second of the day together. As soon as they are separated from the pack, they are in acute danger of dying. This is especially true for puppies. They could never survive alone and need their pack. Keep in mind that your puppy fears for his life if he is alone. At least in the first attempts.

So, you should never leave him alone for an hour and think that he is already getting used to it. This would be a disaster for your relationship and the well-being of your dog.

 The very first step in staying alone is actually not closing the apartment door behind you, but leaving a room. Many puppies get used to always running after their mistress or master in the apartment. In the first days this is ok. Your dog does not know his new home yet and has to settle in first. He is looking for your proximity. After a few days you should start to chase your dog away. Because if your dog can't even stay alone in a room, he won't be able to stay alone in the apartment.

If you have a puppy that is constantly chasing you, you can just really annoy him. You run back and forth in the apartment until your puppy lies down in his bed by himself. You do this exercise several times a day until your puppy doesn't start running after you anymore.

When you are at that point, you can start leaving him alone in the apartment. You should definitely avoid making a big drama. There is no goodbye, the dog is not cuddled. Without a word you leave the apartment, close the door behind you and move away from the door a long way. Moving away from the door is important because otherwise your dog will know that you are still standing in front of it. After all, he perceives your smell.

For example, you can bring in the mail. The first time, you should leave your dog alone for a minute at most.

After that you come back inside. Don't make a big drama out of it either. You can say hello to him for a moment and then immediately sit down on the couch and relax until your dog has calmed down. On this day you should leave your puppy alone several times for about one minute. You do this for several days until your dog is completely relaxed.

Next, you can slowly extend the times. Make sure that you do not take too big steps and do not overstrain your dog. However, if you manage to get your puppy to be alone for half an hour, an hour will not be a problem.

No matter how well you train him to be alone, your dog still needs your closeness. A dog should never be left alone for more than six to seven hours. After all, he has to do his business and wants to be kept busy.

## Getting a grip on hunting behavior

Every dog has hunting in its blood. After all, this is their natural food source. Some dogs hunt more, some less. To get a dog with a low hunting instinct, you should look at the different dog breeds. After all, there are dog breeds that were bred for hunting. These are of course much stronger hunters. To stop the hunting behavior, you have to intervene early. The hunting behavior includes locating, fixing, sneaking, chasing, packing, killing, tearing and eating the prey. Most dogs show only some parts of the hunting behavior and not the whole process.

A first sign of hunting behavior is when the dog pricks up its ears, tenses its body, and looks concentrated in a certain direction. Your dog has noticed something there and tries to locate the prey. As soon as he knows where it is, he rushes after it. If you only try to intervene when your dog is already running, you are too late. You have to intervene as soon as he locates the prey.

Already at puppy age you should stop the hunting behavior of your dog. Otherwise it becomes a big problem at an advanced age. In order to control the hunting behavior, you should teach your dog the command "Stay". You start off very simply and then add more and more stimuli that your dog has to resist.

Besides suppressing the hunting instinct, you should also give your dog the opportunity to live out his instincts but under controlled conditions.

This works best with a food bag. With this you can teach your dog how to retrieve. If your dog prefers to sniff to find its prey, you can hide the food bag and let your dog search for it. These activities will help you to keep your dog busy. A busy dog is less inclined to hunt than a bored dog.

Besides all these things, the recall is also crucial. This must work perfectly so that you can call your dog off in almost any situation, even from hunting.

**Safe outdoors without injuries**

A dog that lives in the city should be reasonably roadworthy. Only very few dogs can walk on the street without a leash. However, it is beneficial for every dog to be prepared at the street. After all, it can always happen that a dog wiggles itself out of its harness or collar. Or maybe your dog runs near a street while you have not leashed him.

For your dog to be able to walk unleashed along a road, the recall must work perfectly. In addition, your dog must have internalized stopping at the curb and crossing the street on command. It is important that your dog be used to cars, trucks, bicycles, motorcycles and all other vehicles. He should also show no hunting behaviour towards vehicles. Right from the start you should make sure that your dog stops at the street. In the beginning you just walk beside the cars so that your puppy gets used to it. When you want to cross the street for the first time, let your dog sit. As soon as you give the command, you run across the street. This is a procedure that you consistently follow. This way your dog learns that he may only cross a street when you give the command. The aim is for your dog to stop and sit down by the street on its own. Remember that your dog should always sit on the curb. This is a limit he can understand.

If you are on a road that is blocked by cars so that you cannot see from the curb if a car is coming, leave your dog waiting at the curb while you go ahead and see if a car is coming. The dog is not allowed to cross the road until you give the command. When this procedure is instilled in your dog, you can feel safe.

Especially in the darker seasons you should make sure your dog is clearly visible. Put a glowing collar or coat on him so that your puppy can be seen by cars and other road users

If you do all these things, your dog will be perfectly prepared for the city and will be able to move pretty safely between cars. But can you now let your dog walk on streets without a leash?

Only you can decide that for yourself. How much do you trust your dog not to run into the street?
If all these training steps are learned perfectly, you can let him run without a leash. Be aware, however, that no matter how well your dog is trained, mistakes can always happen. Therefore, you can never be one hundred percent sure that your dog will not run into the street, but good training still offers you a lot of security.

## Prevent and train off feed aggression

Some dogs tend to develop feeding aggressions. This
is a behavior that is absolutely sensible in nature.
After all, the dog has to look at how he gets his food.
In pet keeping, however, this is a very undesirable
behavior. After all, your dog gets enough to eat. Food
aggression only causes stress between dogs.
Sometimes these aggressions can even be directed
against humans. The good thing is, this behavior is not
yet present in the puppy. So, you can easily prevent
this behavior and you will never have any problems
with it. If your puppy is still very young, you should
get him used to having the bowl taken away from him
from time to time, and then giving it back to him. But
you should do this only rarely. Otherwise, your dog
may be very stressed when he eats because he is afraid
you will take his food away again. This can lead to
food aggression. Take the food away from him only
very rarely and give it back to him afterwards.

If your dog tries to growl when you reach for the food
bowl, you should not be intimidated by it and take the
bowl away anyway. Otherwise your dog will notice
that the growling will help him succeed in this case

and the feeding aggression that we wanted to avoid will develop.

If you got your dog from a good breeder, you don't have to worry that your puppy will bite you because he has learned good social behavior.

**Getting used to nibbling on furniture**

Nibbling and biting are quite normal behaviors of puppies. They explore their world and get to know things. He also uses his teeth to keep them clean and healthy. Even an adult dog should therefore chew on things from time to time. This keeps the teeth healthy. If you bring a puppy into your house, you must expect that your furniture will suffer from it. You should definitely be aware of this. If you bring a dog into your house, you have to expect dirt, hair and even some scratches in the furniture. However, you can still stop your dog from chewing furniture. The first step, of course, is to build up a bite inhibition.

Then there are some small things you should pay attention to. Your dog must be fed sufficiently and have enough exercise and rest periods. In this way you will satisfy the needs of your dog and he will be satiated, working to capacity, but not stressed.

The most important thing is to offer alternatives. Your dog should always have chewing toys available. As soon as you catch him chewing on a piece of clothing or furniture, stop him and offer him a chew toy instead. With a lot of patience, you will eventually manage to get your dog to leave your furniture alone.

**Protection against toxic bait**

Unfortunately, we also have to talk about this. It is terrible that poisoned bait exists at all. They are laid out by mentally and socially impaired people who have an exaggerated aversion to dogs. They prepare liver, sausage, or other delicacies with fishhooks, razor blades or rat poison. The aim is that the dog that eats this poisonous bait dies from it. And unfortunately, some poison baits have been successful.

Of course, you want to prevent your dog from getting such a poisonous bait. Therefore always stay up to date. Word gets around quickly among dog owners when poisoned bait has been laid out in a certain area.

There is even an app that you can download. There you can see all the poisoned baits that have been found. Stay away from these areas to avoid unnecessary danger. All dogs are exposed to the danger of poisoned bait because they are always looking for food, and as soon as they find something, they swallow it. You must be especially careful with puppies and young dogs because they are much more curious and naive than older dogs.

If you want to make sure that your dog is not caught by a poisonous bait, you can do a poisonous bait training with him. Teach your dog that he must not pick up food from the ground. You will need a lot of patience for this exercise, because it is very unnatural for dogs not to devour found food immediately. It is a great help if you have already taught your dog impulse control, and if he can also master a termination command. This allows you to intervene in an emergency.

However, there is one more nice exercise that might be fun for both of you. You teach your dog to display the found food instead of eating it. To practice this behavior, you hide a great treat and watch your dog closely. Once he has found the food, you praise him effusively and leave him sitting. Then you give him another treat that your dog likes even better. You have to repeat this exercise several times. If your dog is voracious and has the food in his mouth before you have had a chance to praise him, you can use an aid. A fruit basket or a baker's basket, whatever you can find, can help you do this exercise. The important thing is that it is an object with holes that you can place over the food. Your dog will try to get to the food first. As soon as he comes to rest, you let him sit or make room and reward him.

He does not get the food under the basket because that is the point of the exercise. If you feel safe, you can leave the baskets out. It is aloe important that your dog does not find food on the floor.

When you do this training, you must always keep your dog on a leash. If you let him run free, he might find food and that would jeopardize your training. If you do this training for a while, you will quickly see results. In the future, your dog should always sit down when he finds a piece of food. For this he will get a special reward. When you get there, your training is finished.

The difficulty here is that you always have to keep a good eye on your dog. If you turn away for a few seconds and don't see your dog showing you a piece of food, he might decide to eat it after all. To prevent this from happening, you can teach your dog to indicate the food by barking.

You can teach him any behavior you want. You can also make your dog do a roll or jump in the air. Whatever you want. Of course, you only teach the dog what does not harm him.

Now let's learn how to teach the most important commands.

# Basic Commands - Teach the First Commands Very Easily

The basic education your puppy should have is very extensive. After all, your puppy is like a blank page. You have to find the right words and techniques to do everything right from the beginning. If you teach your dog this basic education, you will have a perfectly trained dog that many will envy you for. But this requires a lot of work. And in addition to all the basic training, your dog should also know a few commands. The commands explained in this chapter are important for the education of your dog. Therefore, he should be able to understand them. However, there are many more commands that he can learn. For example, teaching "give paw" or "nod" is just to make your dog work his head and you two have fun together. You should therefore teach your dog commands for the rest of his life to challenge him again and again. The first

commands in this chapter that your dog should learn
are an important part of the training.


## When is it time for the first training?

You can start training quite early. House training
starts on the first day and you can also introduce some
other educational measures on the first day.
But do not overdo it. Because on this day your puppy
was separated from his family and came to a
completely new environment. This is a lot for him to
get used to, so a specific training should not take
place on this day yet. He has to settle in first. In the
first night you can still be considerate with your dog
and spend the night together with him. This closeness
is important. House training continues at night. As
soon as he gets nervous, he goes outside to do his
business. If you want, you can teach your dog a
command on the first day. This is even advisable,
because this way you can keep your dog busy, which
strengthens the bond. You also distract him from the
thoughts of his dog family and make it easier for him
to separate. You can start with an easy training. Do
not make the first training too long. Five to ten

minutes are quite sufficient on the first day. You can increase this over time.


**How do I recognize that my puppy is overwhelmed?**

When you bring your very first puppy into the house, you are probably full of good intentions and want to do everything right. This can quickly lead to you overtaxing your puppy by trying to teach him too many commands at once or by making the training sessions too long. If this happens, your dog will not be able to concentrate well and will not enjoy the training as much. Five to ten minutes is quite sufficient for a young puppy. You should only practice one command at a time. One of the first things your dog should learn besides house training is his name because the most important thing is that he reacts to it.

Since every dog is different, it is very important that you get to know the character of your puppy. Sensitive dogs are overwhelmed faster than self-confident dogs. You have to take this into account. That's why there are no general guidelines on how long a dog has to be mentally and physically challenged each day.

You must therefore pay attention to the signs coming from your dog. If he is overwhelmed with your training, he could show this by the following behavior:

- Yawn

- Shake (Dogs often do this to shake off stress)

- Restlessness and nervousness

- Bite the line

- Constant scratching (check first to see if your dog has fleas or other parasites)

- Panting at cool temperatures

- Frequent licking and nibbling

- Loss of appetite

Individually these behaviors can indicate a disease or be absolutely harmless. However, if your dog is perfectly healthy and yet repeatedly displays several of these behaviors, you may be overtaxing your dog.

There are also signs that you are not keeping your dog busy enough. These include:

- Groundless and frequent barking

- Chasing his own tail

- Scratched furniture, frayed carpets, dug up flower beds and other mischief

- Aggression

- Apathetic behavior (if neglected for too long)

Under- and overstraining should be avoided in dog keeping. Of course, it can happen that you do not satisfy your dog's needs sufficiently or too much for one day. This is not a big deal. We humans sometimes feel the same way. However, you should react to this and adjust your training schedule. Under no circumstances should your dog suffer permanently from over- or underchallenge because otherwise it could cause permanent damage.

But now we start with the most important commands.

## No

The "no" is a command that every dog should be able to master. It is the so-called abort signal. This can be as loud as you want. You can also call "Pfui" or "Stop" or whatever. The important thing is that you train it properly. You can also train two different signals. One to tell your dog not to eat something (impulse control) and one to stop if he is already eating.

You can easily train the first signal by positive amplification. You take a piece of food in your hand, hold it out to your dog and say your command. The dog will want to take the food because he does not know the signal yet. Then your hand will close. It will remain closed until your dog has come to rest. Then you open your hand again and say your command. As soon as the dog wants to go back to the food, the hand closes. Repeat this procedure until your dog has understood that he is not getting the food.
If he does not take the food even though your hand is open, praise him and give him a treat from the other

hand. This can be a very special and better treat. This enhances the effect. Because the dog learns that he gets something even better if he listens to you.

Do this training a few times every day. Depending on how patient your dog is, he will internalize it quickly or less quickly. Here again your patience is needed. Your dog needs time, because impulse control is really difficult for dogs. If you have taught your dog this signal with a lot of patience, he will be much easier to control in the future. You can forbid him to eat a piece of food, but you have to see it yourself in time. Sometimes you do not succeed because our dogs have good noses and sometimes sniff things that are not recognizable to us as food. If your dog is already eating, your dog may not obey the impulse control signal. This always depends on how greedy your dog is. If he listens to your signal when he eats, everything is fine. Then you don't need a second one.

However, if your dog does not respond, you will have to work more to rehearse an abort signal. You place a large bowl of food in front of your dog. During the first training, fill the bowl with food your dog does not like to eat anyway. He could of course eat it any way, but it should not be too hard for him to stop. It should also be small pieces of food so that your dog doesn't devour everything at once. Let your dog eat. After a short time, you will give your abort signal. Your dog will most likely not stop eating. In this case you give him a slight push in the neck area. Of course, you must not hurt him. This is only a slight push to make your dog understand that his behaviour was wrong. The first time you should be especially gentle with the reprimand, because some dogs are very sensitive.

If you know how your dog reacts to this, you can always increase the reprimand. You take the bowl away and wait a few seconds. After a while, put the bowl down and let the dog eat again. It is possible that your dog will then no longer dare to eat because he has been discouraged. If this is the case, you can vary the measure a little and give your dog another bowl of food or give the food out of your hand. This is because he should relate the task specifically to your signal.

Do this training only two or three times in a row and then let your dog finish everything. He should notice that you do not always interrupt him when he is eating. Give him a break and continue the training a few hours later.

If your dog stops eating the very first time you use the signal, celebrate it and reward it with a very special treat. The fact that he stopped was probably just a coincidence, but if you celebrate him extensively, he may stop at the second sound of the signal. This way you don't have to apply your moderation at all and can teach your dog the abort signal only by positive reinforcement.

Both signals are important, especially if you have a greedy dog with a good nose. You want to be sure you can stop him from eating chocolate and other foods that are very harmful to your dog.

**Come**

This command refers to the reliable call back. This is critically important. Every dog should be given the opportunity to move freely without a leash, but this is only possible if he comes back to you when you call him. This is not only important for you, but especially for other people. There are people who are afraid of dogs and do not want to be jumped on. There are people with guide dogs. If the guide dog is distracted by your dog, he could make a mistake that could cost his owner his life.

In many situations it is important to be able to retrieve your dog. This does not mean that your dog comes when he is just standing around; he must also come when there are lots of distractions. This is the very highest level of control over your dog, and very difficult to train. If you choose to use a word signal, you have the problem that your voice sounds very different when you are angry or excited. This can also affect your dog in whether he comes or not. The better option is therefore the dog whistle. It always sounds the same.

How do you train using the whistle? The first thing your dog needs to understand is that after the whistle comes a reward. Since this is one of the most difficult signals for the dog to understand, you should also dig out the best treat you can find. This is only for coming back and at no other time so that it will remain something very special.
You sit down in front of your dog with the treat and hold it out to him. Your hand closes again and again

when the dog wants to take it. At some point he will understand that he must not take it. Then you give your signal and hold the treat closer to your dog. He will take it. You do this exercise 20 to 30 times a day. Your dog will soon link the treat to the signal.
The goal is that you give him the treat and he turns his head right away because he knows that otherwise he can't have it. When you give the signal, your dog jumps on the food without you even moving your hand. He should only react to the signal.

Next, you can call your dog in the apartment from time to time. For example, when you go to the bathroom, call your dog with the signal. As soon as he comes, he will get the special treat and lots of praise. You can also use this calling outside.

But be careful. There is no measure for this signal. If you reprimand your dog after the signal sounds because he has not come, you will poison the signal. It is no longer purely positive and your dog does not feel the need to come to you. In other words, if your dog does not come, there is nothing you can do. You should therefore only use the signal when you are sure that your dog will come.  If it happens once or twice that your dog does not hear, it is not the end of the world. However, as soon as it happens more often, your dog will learn that he can simply ignore the signal. You must therefore proceed using very small steps.

If your dog hears it well with slight distractions, you can go one step further. You should take this step in the apartment first. Find a bigger distraction in the form of a particularly good smelling food or a particularly nice toy and try to call your dog. As soon as this works well, you can go one step further and do it outside at some point.

Patience is incredibly important. Until your dog responds perfectly to the call back, a lot of time will pass. But when it finally happens, you won't have to worry about it anymore and you can let your dog run free everywhere.

## Sit

The popular sit. Why is that important? With the command, "Sit," you can make your dog relax. You help him settle down by giving him a command. You direct his concentration to you and thus make sure that he relaxes a little. This does not have to be "sitting," and can be anything else. But "sit" is the simplest command. Every dog should be able to master at least one command. Eventually, you can teach your dog several commands. You can teach him up to his mental capacity.

It is even very easy to teach your dog the command "sit." What you should avoid is pressing his bottom down. He will only press against it and you will achieve nothing. Instead, holding a tasty piece of food over his head is much more effective. You hold it so high that he can't reach it and you hold it so far back that your dog automatically sits down to see it. If your dog refuses to sit down, you can easily stroke his bottom and try to push him down a little bit. But as soon as you notice that your dog is pressing against it, you should take your hand away. When your dog sits down, your signal will sound and he will be fed. But the food is only available after you have given the signal.
If you repeat this exercise several times a day, your dog will learn to sit very quickly. You can also use a hand signal to accompany your word signal. Most dogs respond much better to the hand signal than to

the word signal because they generally communicate much more through body language.

**Stay**

The last of the four basic commands is "Stay". This is helpful in many situations. By giving the command you can let your dog know that you will come back. If you go to a restaurant or are in another new environment, your dog may be on your heels. He will follow you everywhere. Sometimes this is really annoying. For example, if you only want to go to the toilet for a short time.

In this case you can simply give your dog the command to stay and he will lie down relaxed because he knows that you will come right back and he will get a reward. It therefore makes life easier for both of you. It is also relatively easy to train. You give your dog the command to stay and walk backwards a few steps away from him. If he remains sitting, you go back to him, praise him and give him a treat. Then you move a little further away. If he remains seated, you go back to him and reward him. You continue to do this until you can even leave the room without your dog running after you.

You have to be absolutely consistent in your training. When your dog gets up and wants to follow you, you take a threatening step towards your dog and bring him back to the same place. Then you give the command again and take a few steps away. Only if the dog remains sitting, well-behaved, will there be a reward. The "stay" is thereby quickly learned.
If you can get out of the room without your dog running after you, you can also add slight distractions and maybe open the refrigerator door or shake the bag of treats. If your dog sits well-behaved, there is a great reward.

# Everything You Should Know About Health, Nutrition & Sleep of the Puppy

## Sleep

We all know that puppies are full of life and mischief! But exploring the world is a tough job, and puppies need plenty of sleep to balance the energy expended during learning. Puppies are like babies and face the same challenges when it comes to understanding the world around them. Like babies, puppies are unlikely to sleep through the night. If they are very young, puppies may wake up to relieve themselves.

It is important to keep an eye on your puppy's sleeping behavior. Did you know that the sleep phases a dog goes through are very similar the human sleep phases? They are:

**Solidification/acceptance**: This is the first phase and corresponds to the transition from the waking state to the sleeping state. It lasts only a few minutes and the dog can react perfectly to external stimuli.

**Light sleep**: In this phase it becomes more difficult for the dog to wake up abruptly, but the brain can still cause sudden physical reactions. The first physiological changes are observed and the heart rate decreases.

**Deep or delta sleep**: Lasts about 20 minutes and is characterized by broad brain waves and a slow breathing rhythm. Dreams are not yet common in this phase.

**REM phase**: This is the phase of rapid eye movement, characterized by very high brain activity that produces dreams. In this phase we can observe the dog moving its legs or ears.

Is it normal that a puppy sleeps a lot?
If your puppy sleeps a lot, it is understandable that you might be worried at first, but this is perfectly normal and does not indicate any disturbance in the

puppy. How much sleep can a puppy get under normal conditions? Until the age of 12 weeks, a puppy will sleep 18 to 20 hours a day, as his body is in a developmental stage, so nutrition and rest are essential for the beginning of a healthy life.

You have to keep in mind that everything is new for a puppy and that it is exhausting for him to absorb all the information gained from the environment. However, from the age of 12 weeks, the puppy gradually becomes more active, so that he integrates new activities (both physical and mental) into his daily life.

Should I wake up the puppy?

Does your puppy not want to wake up even though you touch him gently? Puppies are lovable and it is essential to accept them with love. But even if you feel like cuddling, stroking and holding him all the time, remember that the puppy is a living being with personal needs, not a toy. Under no circumstances should you interrupt your puppy's sleep, because that would be bad for the normal development of his body, which needs a lot of energy to mature all organs and body functions. From the age of 3 months on, you will see that your dog will gradually become more active and will therefore have more time to gradually build up a routine. However, you should not be in a hurry, and respect the normal times for your puppy's development.


**Nutrition**

Breast milk is the ideal initial food for a puppy, as it is rich in all the nutrients that the puppy needs to grow up healthy and strong. Although puppies can be weaned at six to eight weeks of age, most begin to take an interest in solid food at three to four weeks - usually by frolicking in their mother's bowl and licking the food off their paws!

This is the best time to start providing puppy food. If you choose a dry food, add water and puree it into a mash. As the puppy grows, add less water and give him more and more dry food. Don't be tempted to wean your puppy too early, because an early switch to a solid food only diet can affect your puppy's underdeveloped digestive system.

How much food you should give the puppy?

Very often puppies eat more with their eyes than with their stomach (Just like us humans ☺)! To keep the right balance between what he needs and overfeeding, give him small amounts of food more often. This depends on the age, size and recommendations of your veterinarian. Start with a spoonful of food five times a day while your puppy is still suckling, and follow these general guidelines:

- From the beginning of solid food until weaning (usually two months): 4-6 meals per day.

- Two to three months: 4 meals a day.

- Four to six months: 2-3 meals per day.

- After six months: 2 meals per day (depending on the breed).

Don't overload your puppy, because too much food can strain his digestive system or put unnecessary pressure on his skeleton if he gains too much weight in a short period of time. Neither is good for your puppy's health, so be careful when planning his meals. Always read the feeding instructions on the packaging of his food carefully, as they provide a good reference point. The exact amount of food for the puppy may vary according to age, breed, health status and energy level: Playful, active puppies consume more energy, so they need more fuel!

If you weigh your puppy regularly, you can be sure that he has the right weight for his age, size and breed. You can do this at home, but if you're not sure how to do it, ask your vet to teach you or do it for you at an examination.

Do not feed your puppy immediately before or after exercise: Allow an hour to elapse between meal and exercise.

It is a good idea to get the puppy used to resting for a while after feeding to avoid the risk of digestive problems or more serious disorders, especially in larger breeds where the stomach can turn over. This phenomenon is known as "stomach distension and rotation," and is a medical emergency that requires urgent veterinary attention.

**Health**

When you take a puppy into your life, you must pay close attention to ensure that he grows up healthy, both physically, and in terms of behavior, and that he looks good.

Monitor his health at home and consult your vet if there are any warning signs. In principle a healthy puppy is rather playful and self-confident, not shy.

These are indications that your puppy is healthy:

1. Bright eyes, no spots or blemishes.

2. Vigilant, pays attention to noises, turns his head.

3. Clean ears, no unpleasant odors.

4. Clean and healthy skin, no irritated areas, soft hair.

5. Teeth well arranged.

6. No deficits in the posture of the limbs.

7. He should not be fat, even if puppies look like stuffed balls, there is a limit.

8. The faeces must be well defined, without parasites being present.

9. The belly should not protrude too much, because this indicates parasites.

10. In male puppies palpate the testicles. The age at which they come down varies from case to case. It can be between one week and 8 months.

11. During socialization it is extremely important to work on social relationships with both humans and other animals to avoid future behavioral problems.

However, these are only indications. As a layman, I recommend you to visit the vet regularly, especially if one or more of these signs occur.

Now I would like to go into more detail on a few points:

Oral and dental care
Dental problems are quite common in dogs, so one of the best things you can do for him is to brush his teeth. You can buy special dog toothbrushes and toothpaste from your vet (the latter is very important). You should not use any of your own toothpaste; firstly, because your dog will not like the taste (he

will probably like meat more than mint), and secondly, because it makes too much foam.

If you notice bad breath or bleeding gums in your puppy, inform your vet. Teenage puppies have an uncontrollable urge to chew on everything. There are several theories about why they do this, but whatever is right, if you want to keep your favorite slippers, give your puppy things to chew on.

Ear care

You should clean the inside of your puppy's ears at least once a week. Use a different cotton ball for each ear. It's not a good idea to use cotton buds because you might hurt him. Make sure his ears are free of excess wax, secretions, and unpleasant odors. If you suspect that your puppy has ear problems, such as infections, wounds or parasites, do not hesitate to take him to the vet.

Stress in dogs

It may not be the same as a "physical" illness, but if the puppy shows signs of stress, you should be worried.

It is normal for your puppy to whimper at your home during his first nights. After this initial phase, there are other factors that can put a strain on your puppy. Separation stress for example is quite common. Give him lots of love to calm him down. However, if the problem persists or becomes more serious, consult your vet.

Prevention is better than cure
Your puppy should have received his first vaccinations before he came to you and the breeder or shelter should give you a document to prove this. The best thing you can do for your puppy's health is to stick to the vaccination schedule. It is also very important to deworm your puppy regularly and have him checked for fleas.

Remember that your dog cannot tell you that he feels bad, so it is up to you to figure it out. Worrying external signs are sudden loss of appetite, mood swings, rapid weight loss or gain, lumps or swelling, vomiting, diarrhea and any eye or ear problems.

I have repeated it several times and you should take it seriously: If something is wrong with your dog, go to the vet!

# How Your Puppy Finds True Friends

### Contact with other dogs

It is important that your puppy have contact with other dogs. After all, you want to raise a well socialized dog and this can only be done if you let him get to know different dogs. He has to get to know different breeds of dogs, males, females, old and young dogs. Besides, your dog will have a lot of fun playing around with his fellow dogs. And you will enjoy watching him do so.

However, your puppy is still very young and sensitive. He learns incredibly quickly in this sensitive time. Negative and positive experiences are memorized rapidly. Therefore, you have to make sure that your dog has only positive experiences with other dogs. Otherwise you will raise an anxious and antisocial dog. If you let your puppy have contact with other dogs, you must always keep an eye on your dog and observe him well. The sentence, "They'll work it out between themselves," is absolutely not appropriate here. You must not yet equate these young dogs with adult, experienced dogs. In puppy age, dogs are very similar to children. They do not yet know what is right and wrong, and sometimes they behave like real bullies.

If you notice that your dog is afraid or is being bullied by other dogs, bring your dog to you and offer him protection. That way he learns that he can trust you. In order to recognize if your dog is feeling bad, you must look into the behavior of dogs. As soon as your dog shows fear through his body language or seeks protection from you, you should offer him that protection. But you can also see from the play of the dogs whether everything is alright. When your dog is having fun, his body is relaxed. He moves joyfully back and forth. His whole body is curvy and soft. When playing is relaxed, all movements are exaggerated. Dogs make grimaces, let their tongues hang out, roll over on the floor and jump around like crazy.

An important sign of a friendly game is role reversal. If other dogs always attack your dog, you should step in between them. When dogs take turns being chased, you know that it is a pleasant game for all of them. Even short interruptions are part of the game. The dogs take their time to come down so that the game does not escalate into aggression and remains fun. A clear sign for a game is also the game challenge. On this occasion, the dog puts its front paws on the ground and stretches its bottom in the air. If he takes this position, he definitely wants to play .

In the beginning it is very difficult to see if the dogs are playing with each other or not. You simply do not have a trained eye for this when you are a dog beginner. That is quite normal. After some time, you will know exactly what you have to pay attention to. If you are still unsure, you can call in experienced dog owners or a dog trainer for help. It is important that you pay attention to how your puppy feels when he comes into contact with other dogs. If you don't help your dog during this sensitive time, he will have a hard time building up trust in you. In the worst case, he could even suffer a trauma and avoid other dogs in the future. He could permanently develop into a fearful dog if he has a lot of negative experiences in these young years.

Of course, your dog should meet other dogs. But this should only take place in a controlled way so that he has a good time. After all, you wouldn't just throw your children into a group full of strange children you don't know.

**The puppy group**

The puppy group is one of the most popular ways to let the puppy make contacts. If you do not know what this is yet, here is a short explanation. A puppy group is led by a dog trainer who brings several puppies together and lets them play with each other. This is a good idea because older dogs often won't have anything to do with a small lively puppy. This is too much excitement for them. So, if you don't have any puppies in your neighborhood, a puppy group is a nice alternative. Your young dog can have a good romp and meet friends his own age. This does not mean, of course, that your dog should not have contact with older dogs. Your puppy needs to get to know all kinds of dogs of all ages. Older dogs are also very good at showing the little puppy his limits.

If you want to send your puppy to a puppy group, you should look for good quality. Not every puppy group is beneficial for your dog.

In a good puppy group, you will get a theoretical introduction at the beginning, where you can also ask questions. That gives you a little bit of security. The puppies should all be similar in age. Usually the puppies should be between 8 and 16 weeks old. Obviously all puppies in this group must be healthy and vaccinated.

In a good group of dogs, a trainer should not supervise more than 5 - 6 puppies. Otherwise it is difficult even for the trained trainer to supervise all the puppies sufficiently. Also in a puppy group, it is nice if there is an older dog. The mature dog can help the trainer supervise the group and to put the little dogs in their place.

A puppy group session should not last longer than 60 minutes. During this time the puppies should not play continuously. It is much better if the trainer interrupts the game with short obedience exercises.

Of course you should also pay attention to the qualifications of the dog trainer. It is especially good if a trial lesson is offered. You can see if the trainer works with modern educational methods and if you agree with how he treats the dogs.

Just because he calls himself a dog trainer, you don't have to agree with everything he does. If you feel uncomfortable with an exercise, you should address this directly. After all, it is your puppy.

This is probably the most important thing you should consider when looking for a good dog school: Does the dog trainer treat his dogs appropriately?

If you consider these points, a puppy group is a good thing. You can visit them twice a week. It should not be more often, because you don't want to overtax your puppy. There your dog can learn how to deal with other dogs and how to play properly. It is especially important that your puppy meets dogs of different breeds there. By doing so you make sure that your dog does not become racist.

## Puppy protection

Puppy protection actually exists. However, this is valid only in their own herd. With wolves, puppy protection usually only occurs up to the eighth week. When you get your puppy, he is therefore already out of the puppy protection phase.

Puppy protection means that boorish behavior of the puppies is tolerated by the older dogs, because it is a puppy. Many dog owners assume that this puppy protection applies to every dog, but it has been proven that this puppy protection is only valid in their own pack. Dogs within the pack where the puppy grows up actually show a behavior that can be called puppy protection. But as previously stated, this only lasts until about the eighth week. The adult dogs will not permanently tolerate the antisocial behavior of a puppy. This why a puppy must be reprimanded for bad behavior; he has to be taught his limits.

Sometimes an owner gets frightened when an older dog growls angrily at his young puppy. However, this does not mean that the older dog is antisocial. He just showed the young dog his limits. This is important to make him compatible with other dogs.

If you are outdoors with your puppy, you should not expect that he will experience any puppy protection. He will be perceived by other dogs as a strange dog and will be reprimanded if he misbehaves. However, if your puppy does not understand the reprimand and keeps annoying the older dog, you should stop him. If your puppy annoys the older dog too much and doesn't react to threats, it is possible that the older dog will bite.

If you see an adult dog that reacts calmly to your puppy, it has nothing to do with puppy protection. Many adult dogs with a good upbringing put up with the boorish behavior of puppies because they have experienced that they can cope better with it. This does not mean, however, that they are not annoyed by the puppy. You should not allow your puppy to stress other dogs too much, especially if the dog has already made a threat, because there is no puppy protection even for your sweet dog.

When you meet other dogs for the first time, you should be particularly attentive. It is best to keep the puppy on a leash. That way you can stop him when he gets too rough. You should also ask the other owner how his dog reacts to puppies. Some dogs don't know what to do with the tempestuous and boisterous type of puppy, and react quickly and aggressively. Such negative experiences can become a big problem for your puppy. If the dogs get along well, they can meet each other without a leash, but they should still be watched carefully. Pay attention to the difference in size between the dogs. A big dog sometimes does not know his own strength. He can hurt a much smaller dog even though he didn't mean to. You should not intervene immediately in case of a reprimand. This is a good way for your puppy to learn. But as soon as you suspect a danger for your puppy, you should intervene.

Although your puppy will not enjoy puppy protection with older dogs, it is still important that he has regular contact with them. If you only visit puppy groups, this will not be enough to socialize your dog well.
Of course, it is especially helpful if your puppy has contact to well-trained dogs because he will learn a lot from them. With badly trained dogs it is possible that your puppy will learn some negative behavior.

# Children & Puppies - Living Together Peacefully

When children are in the family and a new puppy is brought in, complications can quickly arise. Children first have to learn how to deal with the sensitive being. At a very young age children are sometimes still very rough with pets, which could become a problem.

Your child must understand how the dog expresses itself and how it shows its limits. He must also be aware that he must not kick, hit, or pull the dog's coat. The dog must also respect the child in the family and it must learn that children move differently than adults. Children are dynamic, make fast movements and loud noises. That means you have to get your child used to the dog, and your puppy used to your child. It is not always easy to have a child and a puppy in the same household. But it can have a lot of advantages at the same time. When children help taking care of a dog, they learn to take responsibility. You must never think that you can leave your child completely in charge of the dog. When a dog moves in, the parents must always help with the care.

When a child takes care of a dog, it increases his empathy. He learns how to handle animals and understand the cycle of life. A puppy also brings a lot of energy into the household. Your children will have a lot of fun with their new pet and will be more active.

**The first encounter**

In the beginning it is best to slowly introduce the child to the dog, but then the dog can decide for itself whether it wants to take the last few steps and sniff the child. In this way you will not push your puppy into a situation that is too much for him. You should teach your child from the beginning that he should make a closed fist to sniff. This prevents the dog from biting your child's fingers. You should explain to your child exactly where it is allowed to pet the dog. Since children are not always particularly careful, they should not pet the dog in sensitive areas. The belly, the ears, the tail and the feet are taboo. You should tell your child to stroke the puppy only on the head and neck. You need to make it clear to your child that he must never pull the skin or coat of the dog. He must understand that the dog has the same feelings as another child.

Caution is called for. Depending on how old the child is, it can be difficult to teach him or her this. If your child has just been born, this is not the best time to get a puppy, because an infant is excitement enough.

At the age of about 5 to 6 years, a child is mature enough to understand how to deal with the puppy. When your child and your puppy meet for the first time, it is best to do this in a neutral environment. Treats and toys are taboo. They will cause the dog to be over excited and he might eventually snap, which will scare the child. The child should not be alone with the puppy, neither at the first meeting nor at all other meetings afterwards. There are far too many unwanted things that could happen.

## Baby and puppy in one household

It is not necessarily advisable to get a puppy when a baby has just been born. But of course this depends on the individual situation. If you have decided that it works for you, that is perfectly fine. If you want to get a dog, an older dog is more suitable in this situation, as puppies require much more attention. Especially the command "No" can be very helpful when your baby and the dog meet.

If you already have a puppy and a baby is coming into the family, you must be careful that your puppy does not associate the new family member with negative thoughts. If the baby comes home and you have much less time for the puppy from that point on, he might connect that with the baby. This can cause jealousy. Therefore you should try not to treat your puppy differently than before. Necessary changes should be introduced before the baby shows up. For example, the dog must learn that not everything on the floor is his toy. And it is imperative that he listens when you forbid him to do something.

You can put a baby blanket on the floor where your baby can play. This is taboo for the dog. He is not

127

even allowed to put a paw on it. This is the baby's safety zone and the dog must respect this. It is best to do this before the baby is even there.

One mistake that many people make when they have a baby in the house is they let their dog sniff the baby's diapers and clothes beforehand so that he can get used to the new family member. By this behavior you tell your dog that he has responsibility for the baby. This could lead to him defending the baby, but also to reprimands. If the baby cries, the dog may feel that he has to do something. But since he doesn't know what to do, this causes him a lot of stress. During the first weeks you should keep the baby away from your dog. He is allowed to be close by, but he is not allowed to go to the baby.

This way he understands that you are the parent and take full responsibility. When you allow your dog to get to know the baby, it must be controlled. As soon as the dog learns to approaches the baby slowly and carefully, you should praise him.

If you want your dog to stay away from certain areas of the house in the future, dog guards can help. If you are busy with the baby, you should provide your dog with a toy. Also, your dog should not suffer from boredom or frustration. This will lead to negative behavior.

If you are unable to find enough time for the dog with your new baby, you should employ a dog walker or ask a friend or family member for help. Of course, you must never leave your baby alone with the dog. That is still much too risky.

## Rules in living together with the dog

Rules are enormously important in the education of dogs and children. They can also make living together easier. Since children often do not understand the body language of dogs well, you should set clear rules. The dog must not be touched or called while drinking or eating. He should have absolute peace and quiet. In addition, there should be a basket or a box in which the dog can, rest. If he lies down in it, he must also not be touched or called. If the dog is sleeping, he must not be woken up. Annoying the dog must be absolutely forbidden. Tell your child very clearly that he must not pinch the dog, pull its tail or coat, kick it, or blow in its face.

You must also make it clear to your child that the growl of the dog is a clear sign that he wants to be left alone.

Show your child how to play properly with the dog when he or she is old enough to do so. You can make the rule that your child should play with the puppy once or twice a week. It is also very important to walk the dog and children together.

But not only your child must be given boundaries. Your dog must also understand the taboo zones. For example, you should make it clear to him that he must not jump into the bed of the children. Maybe even the whole room is a forbidden zone. For small children, you can make the play blanket off limits for the dog. You have to make sure that your dog is well behaved. He must listen to the basic commands and obey them. It is especially important that he understands that everyone in the family belongs to the pack and must be respected, even the children. You can also teach your children how to earn respect from the dog.

## The age of the child plays a role

You can involve your child in the education of the dog. This makes life easier for everyone. But of course it depends on the age of the child. At under 10 years of age, you should not leave your child alone with a puppy. This is because children at this age are often not sensitive enough to handle the dog properly. However, the children may be able to feed the dog or give him a treat, but this is only possible if the dog is not too boisterous. A young puppy is usually not yet calm enough. He could knock the child over if he is too excited.

If you think that your child is mature enough, you can allow him to play with the dog. He can throw a ball to the dog, hide treats, or teach him a trick. Every child develops differently. In the beginning, you are always there for the occasional game, and at some point, you may even trust your child to play on his own.

With children and dogs, the question often arises as to when the child can walk the dog alone. There is no legal requirement as to when a child may walk the dog by himself so you have to make the decision yourself. It is best if your child often accompanies you on the walks. This will teach him a lot about the dog and the right behavior in difficult situations. You can let your child lead the dog while you accompany them. Once you feel comfortable with it, you can send your child off on his own.

It is important that you go through every possible situation with your child because unforeseen situations can always arise. Your child must be prepared for these.

Restricted dogs are dogs that the law classifies as dangerous. Anyone who owns such a dog must have a dog handler license, for which you must be 16 years of age or older. Children under this age are not allowed to take a restricted dog for a walk alone.

# A Well-Behaved Puppy
# With or Without Dog School

**Is dog school a must?**

In other words: Why do we go to dog school?
Dog training is very complex, much more complex
than you might think at the beginning because a dog
is a highly social being. It needs a gentle, but firm
education. This is not easy if you have no experience
with dogs; therefore many people rely on a dog
school.

However, there is a lot of information online and in
books that can help you become the best dog trainer
for your dog. This book is an example. You will also
learn a lot from your dog himself. After all, this is
how you do it with the education of your children.
You read up, get advice from experienced parents, and
blend it with your own ideas.

133

If you do everything right from the beginning and train your dog with much love, you will probably not have any major problems. However, it is also quite normal for you to be insecure in the beginning. Therefore, you may want to get advice from a professional. Strange rumors often circulate among dog owners and the advice often differs. That's why you might want advice from a professional who tells you exactly what is right and what is wrong.

However, this is not so simple, because the methods of dog trainers can also be different. Each person has different ideas about correct dog training. Sometimes you come across a dog school where a leash jerk is used specifically as a training method or the alpha litter is used. Some dog trainers are rough with the dogs and use training methods that you might not be comfortable with.

You cannot expect to go to a dog training school and get the right answers to all your questions. Dog training is not that simple. You must learn for yourself which training methods work best for you and your dog. A good trainer can  be helpful with these things.

Before you go to a dog school, you should inform yourself about them. Look at reviews and get opinions from other people who have been there before. Look at the website and pay attention to the training methods the dog training school describes. Sometimes a dog trainer or a dog school also advertises itself through a podcast or a YouTube channel. There a trainer tells about everyday problems with his "students" and how he solves them. In this way you can already determine whether you like the trainer and whether you agree with his training methods.

Before you book a training session, the trainer should offer you a consultation so you can get to know each other and you can explain your wishes. You can also ask about the trainer's certification. It is important that the trainer continues his training on a regular basis so that he does not get stuck with outdated training methods.

So, you can't rely on a dog school to automatically solve all problems and teach your dog everything. You must determine what is best for you and your dog. But if you are unsure, a well-chosen dog school can help you.

Some dogs also develop problems at an advanced age. These begin inconspicuously at first. Your dog runs after a cyclist. You don't worry about it until a few weeks later when your dog has developed a strong hunting instinct towards cyclists and you don't know what to do about it. There are also dogs that naturally have a strong hunting instinct. With some difficult behaviors, a dog owner reaches his limits.

In this case a good dog school can help. But always be aware that a dog trainer will only show you the training methods. You must enforce them. A visit to a dog school is not a miracle pill, but only a support.

If you would like to go to a dog school with your puppy, you should wait at least one week before doing so. Your puppy must first settle into his new home before you take him to a dog school.

# Punishment Without Violence!

A puppy learns best through positive reinforcement. We humans tend to let our dog consciously make mistakes and then punish him for them. We assume that this is a good way to show the dog what kind of behaviour we want.

The best way to reinforce a positive behavior is before he makes a mistake. This way the puppy will have a lot of fun in training and will learn much better. Nevertheless, no training can be done without punishment. Here you should distinguish between appropriate and inappropriate punishments.

In dog training, it is especially important that you give your dog feedback immediately after his behavior. If you want to punish your dog, you must do so immediately after his behavior. If you wait for an hour or even a few minutes, your dog will not be able to make a connection to his behavior. However, you do not have to inflict physical pain on your dog to punish him; that is exactly what you should not do. After all, you don't want to mistreat your dog, you want to educate him. There are much milder methods of punishment that are much more successful and do not endanger your relationship.

A punishment can be a big problem for the relationship with your dog. Your dog wants to be able to rely on you, and he can only do that if you are predictable for him. If he does not understand what he is being punished for, you are unpredictable for him and he trusts you less. It is the same with severe punishments. Your dog might become scared of you.

When you punish your dog, you should proceed carefully and always be specific. Arbitrary punishments are useless. If you are unsure, it is better to do nothing at all. You will not cause any harm. Next time when you are better prepared, you will be able to react more appropriately. The punishment always depends on the behavior of your dog. You always have to analyze why your dog shows a certain behavior. Far too quickly, a person tends to think that his dog wants to annoy him with this behavior. But this is never the case. The dog lives out his drives and you have to show him what he is and is not allowed to do.

You can do this in a loving and calm way. If you know why your dog behaves in a certain way, you can also praise or punish him appropriately. It works much better if you reward your dog as soon as he shows good behavior.

As already mentioned, you cannot succeed in dog training without punishment. However, you should stick to appropriate punishments. For a dog it is a punishment if you ignore him, put him on a leash, stop the training or game immediately, take a threatening step towards him or use an abort signal. All this seems small to us at first, but dogs are sensitive creatures and react very strongly to this kind of punishment.

# Successful Clicker Training With a Puppy

There are many techniques of dog training, and the clicker is one of them. It is a small device with which you can make a distinctive clicking sound. The dog perceives this sound as a reward.

The noise is produced when the metal sheet is bent in the Clicker. The Clicker is designed so that the sound is always the same and we can use it as often as we want. Nowadays, some clickers are designed to allow us to control the intensity of the sound, which is very useful. Clickers are available at a very low price, they last for many years. They are very easy to use and there are many trainers who use clickers in their daily exercises.

How to use the Clicker?

A clicker is nothing more than an indication to the dog that he has executed the command well, i.e. a way to talk to our dog and tell him that he has done well. The basic idea is to use the Clicker when the dog obeys our command correctly.

Dogs need to understand the click sound as something positive, so we need to teach them to associate the click with a reward. This is a positive reinforcement technique that we need to do for two or three weeks before using the Clicker as a training device.

The easiest way for your dog to associate the click with a reward is to sit on the floor with our dog and just give him some rewards, such as small pieces of sausage.

The principle is:

1.  You make a click with the clicker

2.  You give the dog a reward and praise him.

You don't have to train the puppy to associate the click with a reward. This is done rather subconsciously, without asking anything in return.

That means, for example, we click every half minute or every minute, and then we give our dog a piece of sausage (or some other reward) while we praise him. If the dog practices this at least a couple of times a day, it will only take two or three weeks for the dog to associate the clicking sound with something positive, a reward.

When to use the Clicker?

As soon as you get used to the clicker, you can use it in training. The correct way to use it is to click just when the dog obeys the command. The click is the way to tell your dog "well done" when he has really done it right.

Suppose you train your puppy to lie down when you give this command. The correct way to use the clicker is to click it exactly when the dog lies down on the floor. When he hears a click, he will know he did it well. It may seem a bit strange, but the dog's logic in this case is as simple as that.

Imagine you want to teach your dog to pretend that he is crying or sad. Or in other words, you train him to put his paw in his face. Then follow these steps:

1. Select a word you want to assign to this command. Remember that it must be a word that your dog normally does not hear, otherwise you run the risk that the training will not work.

2. Put something on the dog's mouth that attracts his attention. for example, a Post-it.

3. When you see his paw go up to get it off, say the word you have chosen, for example "sad".

4. Immediately after he has done it, you make the clicker sound.

5. Although in principle the dog should only follow your instructions with the help of the clicker, it is okay to use small treats when you start with a new instruction. This way he will not forget.

Some trainers have the idea that the Clicker is a kind of wonder box that works without the need to feed or play with the dog. Of course, as usual, you have to have realistic expectations

The Clicker is very useful but not absolutely necessary. If you do not have a clicker, you can replace it by clicking with your tongue. To click with your tongue, simply place it on your palate and quickly remove it to click.

# Pay Attention to These 6 Things and Your Puppy Training Will Be 100% Successful

So far, you have learned a lot about the right way to raise your puppy. But there is still a whole lot that can go wrong. Little things can ruin his whole upbringing.

If you have too much information in your head, you can quickly get confused. Therefore, here are a few basic rules. The education is very multifaceted, but if you remember a few basic things, hardly anything can go wrong.

## 1. Leading by example

How do you educate your child properly? You are a good role model. It is the same with your dog. Dogs see their owner as a fully-fledged social partner and therefore watch your behavior patterns with him. You can't be a good role model for an hour a day and otherwise misbehave, because your dog watches you around the clock.

It is very important that you are calm. Your relaxed, balanced posture will transfer to your dog, especially when meeting with strange dogs. If you tense up inside and shorten the leash, your dog will notice this and react immediately.

Be loving to your dog and give him time for everything. If you educate him considerately, he will show the same behaviour towards other people and dogs. Walk with foresight and help your dog if he has problems. If you are generally loving and nice to your dog, he will learn from you. Of course, this is not all that is required to have a well-trained dog. But it is a step in the right direction. If you are a bad example for your dog, you will have a much harder time with training.

## 2. Good socialization

The be-all and end-all in good dog training is socialization. The socialization phase is very important. Slowly introduce him to other dogs and make sure that he makes good experiences. He has to get to know other puppies, adult dogs, old dogs, big and small dogs, and different dog breeds. Always be present and control the meetings so that you can intervene if you notice that it is becoming too much for your dog.

Socialization does not only involve other dogs. Your puppy must also get to know different people; children, babies, old people, injured people and physically handicapped people. Only if he has good experiences with all these different people, will he be relaxed in the future. If your puppy has never really gotten to know children, he might react aggressively to them as an adult dog. This is because children move and behave very differently than adults. The same is true for old and physically challenged people. They walk completely differently and your puppy has to get used to this.

If you have a well socialized dog that is friendly to other people and dogs, it will eliminate a lot of problems in one go, and you'll both live a much calmer life.

## 3. Patience

The most important basic attitude you need for puppy training is patience. Your puppy will put you to the test more than once. In the beginning, he is probably overexcited and needs to be restrained. As soon as he enters puberty, he will again question everything you have already established. Maybe you will have to change your mind about all the rules now.

In these situations, you must remain calm. You must not go crazy and shout at your dog, because you will not achieve anything with that. On the contrary, your dog will no longer take you seriously if you shout at him arbitrarily. Show patience and prove to your dog that you have the leader. Only then will he see you as a true role model and follow your example. When you have gotten through the puppy and teenage years, your patience will pay off. Your adult dog will be a faithful companion who respects you and follows you.

## 4. Rules are important from the beginning

To train your puppy in the best possible way, you have to set up rules right from the beginning. Hopefully this book has made that clear by now. Your puppy is not allowed to move freely everywhere and he does not have constant access to toys and food. If he asks for something and he doesn't get it, he realizes that he is not the center of the world. You have to train your dog in bite inhibition, optimal recall, and many other things.

If you have set enough rules for your dog and taught him the important basics of education, your dog will know that you are the boss. Together with the other facets listed here, you will have a perfectly trained dog. So, apply what you have learned from this book and set appropriate rules.

## 5. Fun and games

Education and bonding are closely linked. If you have a good relationship with your dog, the training will be much easier for you. Your dog wants to train with you and stay close to you because he does not want to lose you.

How to achieve a good bond with your dog is a topic of its own which you have already read about in one of the previous chapters. You have to build trust, communicate properly, and above all, show your dog that he can have fun with you.

That is why you should play with him. Of course every dog is different. Some dogs like to chase a ball, some like to sniff their food, and some like to go jogging.

You have to try different things to find out what your puppy enjoys. There are so many ways to have fun with your dog. Some people are not even aware of what they can do. Do you like riding your bike around? Then you can strap your dog to your bike and make it a shared activity. This could be followed by a small picnic in the park and a bike ride back home, so you can spend a nice day together. If you prefer jogging, you can also take your dog with you. If you or your dog doesn't feel like doing either, you can make your sport a little more exciting.

Have you ever heard of dog dancing? You and your dog learn a dance together. Your dog learns which movement he should make in response to your movements. In the beginning it is certainly very difficult to do this alone at home, so it is a good idea to take a few lessons in a dog school. Make sure that you never practice for more than 15 minutes at a time because that overtaxes him too much.

If dog dancing is not for you, you can also try agility training. You will train on an obstacle course together, and your dog will run over ramps, under bridges, and jump over obstacles, according to your instructions.

Another popular activity is dummy training. You throw your dog a dummy or a food bag. He brings it back to you and you give him a reward. Teaching your dog to retrieve is quite complex. However, once you have succeeded, you can use it in different ways. If you have a dog that likes to run, it is best to throw him the dummy. Or maybe you have a dog that doesn't like to move and prefers to sniff. In this case you can hide the dummy or the food bag and let him look for it. He has to bring it back to you to get a reward.

For a dog that likes to sniff, there are other ways to keep him occupied. For example, you could try man trailing. Your dog is looking for a human. You accompany him with the leash and steer your dog back to the track if he should lose it.

However, you can also give your dog a scent. In doing so, you drag your feet across the ground and drop a piece of food every now and then. At the end of the trail a great reward awaits your dog. Leave the whole thing alone for at least ten minutes, then lead your dog to the start of the trail. There your dog may start sniffing. The treats will show him that your trail is interesting and he should follow it. At the end he receives the big reward. You follow your dog again with the leash so that you can lead him back to the trail if he loses it.

For a better bond with your dog you can also do obedience training. You and your dog do some obedience exercises.

These are just a few examples of what you can do with your dog. If you haven't found the right thing for you, you can do some research. You will surely find a great hobby for both of you. This will strengthen your bond and make the training much easier. Especially during puberty it is very helpful if you spend a lot of time with your dog.

## 6. Protect your furniture

A puppy brings a lot of unbridled energy into your household. You are responsible for directing your dog's energy in the right direction. That's what all the games you play with your dog are for. Nevertheless, it sometimes happens that your dog will take advantage of your furniture. That's why he should have plenty of chew toys available from the beginning. This will enable him to act out his chewing instinct without your furniture suffering.

As soon as your puppy bites or scratch your furniture, you should stop him and offer him a chew toy instead. A reprimand is not necessary. If you consistently prevent him from destroying your furniture and always offer him an alternative, he will quickly create a link and you will hardly have any problems with scratches on your furniture.

When your puppy first comes to lives with you, however, it can happen that a table leg or a couch suffers. If you have a piece of furniture that is particularly important to you, you should protect it. Either you don't let your puppy into the room where the furniture is, or you cover it with plastic sheeting so your puppy can't break it.

You have to expect that one or the other piece of furniture will be a testimony of your puppy's high spirits for a long time. You should be aware of this before your puppy moves in. Only then can you react calmly in these situations. In a household that is too clean and neat, a dog is not welcome anyway. Dogs are messy. They drag a lot of dirt into the apartment and shed their hair everywhere. They also break something now and then. This is something every dog owner has to live with.

## Are there problem puppies?

A puppy is not a blank sheet. He already has many qualities in him. The puppy must fit character-wise into his new family. Otherwise problems can arise quickly. An excited puppy that needs a lot of exercise is usually not a good match with someone who prefers to sit in the apartment all day. That's why it's so important that you think carefully before you buy your puppy.

The word "problem puppy" is no excuse for not training your dog properly. However, some dogs are more easily trained than others. Maybe you have a big problem with your puppy's hunting behavior. Or maybe you just can't get your dog to rest. If you follow all the tips in this book, you will have approached training correctly and for the most part you will have a relaxed and well-trained dog.

A real problem puppy does not exist. You can only create one by not socializing him well. Nevertheless, a behavioral problem may occur that you cannot solve on your own. It is important that you do not despair, because that only leads to you shouting at your dog and that does not bring you success. Stay calm by all means.

If you feel that you are overwhelmed with a behavior of your puppy, you should seek help immediately. The longer you wait, the bigger the problem will be. A good dog school will help you to get the problem under control quickly.

You should definitely remember that no two dogs are alike. Maybe you will never have a certain behavior completely under control. Make friends with the idea that your puppy has an individual personality and you have to come to terms with it. But with the right education you will have a dog that you can control and live with in a relaxed way.

# BONUS: 10 Dog Games for Indoors & Outdoors

Just like us humans, dogs have to keep their minds busy. For this reason, walks and social relationships with other animals and humans are essential to avoid boredom in dogs and to prevent more or less serious behavioral disorders. Stimulating a dog's brain is also a way to make him happier. And playing with the dog is a useful way to train his intelligence.

In this edition of the book I give you 10 games, which are mainly oriented to challenge your dog mentally, a kind of brain jogging. Remember, games and fun are elementary for a puppy. If he learns something at the same time, that is wonderful.

## 1. The hiding game

A hard-working dog is a happy dog. Getting him to carry his own backpack (with his personal belongings) during a walk, or to bring the newspaper home are exercises that train his brain.

Another interesting option is to play hide and seek with him. Smear an object with some moist food and hide it in the park or at home. If the hiding game with the dog takes place in the house, it is preferable to cover the toy with a T-shirt or other old clothes, so the house doesn't get dirty.

The trail may include boxes, cartons and other obstacles that the dog must jump over. The item with the food can be hidden in different places along the trail and when the dog finds it, you reward him with strokes and even some cookies.

## 2. Catch Me If You Can

The dog will enjoy this stimulating and funny dog game. Tie a rope at least 1 meter long to the end of a long stick. At the end of the rope you tie a small cuddly toy. Hide behind a door or wall and hold the stick with your hands while the cuddly toy is lying on the floor, within sight of the dog. If the cuddly toy attracts the dog's attention (you can move the stick slightly for this purpose), the dog will try to catch it with its mouth. At this moment you increase the movement to prevent the cuddly toy from being caught. In this way it becomes a creative game of catching.

### 3. I *smell* something you cannot *see*

Dogs have an extraordinary sense of smell, which is a thousand times superior to that of a human, because its snout has millions of olfactory receptors. Working with this ability is a fun and stimulating game for the dog's brain. It is possible to present new smells to the dog, preferably when they are still very intense, especially during the first few times. Air fresheners from the supermarket, but also fruit, can be a good start.

Let your dog smell the new scent (avoid smells that could cause allergies) and hide it again. Rewards in

the form of caresses calm the dog while he trains his
mind.

## 4. The little bird in the window

Like humans, dogs enjoy new things. If you live in a
house with a terrace or garden, you can put a
birdhouse in front of the window.
This gives the dog varied and entertaining scenery,
which changes accordingly when new birds come in
search of food. This is fun entertainment for the dog,
which helps him not to feel alone.

## 5. Five minutes of music for the dog

Sounds stimulate the dog and are a means of calming
an anxious puppy that suffers when left alone in the
house. Similarly, the calls of wolves or whales in the
sea can stimulate a dog's brain.

The Internet is ideal for finding such sounds for free.
From birds that fly, to farm animals, to other dogs
barking, sounds provide stimulating entertainment for
the dog.

## 6. A new trick!

Teaching your dog a new trick, such as sitting, lying down, or giving paws, is another way to keep the animal's mind active. There are courses and trainers dedicated to teaching dogs, but some homemade tricks can also help and serve to develop the dog's abilities. These training sessions force the dog to keep his brain busy. Increasing complexity is one way to stimulate his mind. You can teach various new tricks to your puppy in a playful way, so that both of you can have a lot of fun.

## 7. The box and the dog

A large, empty cardboard box placed in the middle of a room turns into an exciting game for the dog on rainy days. He can hide in it, you can hide toys in it that he has to look for, and he can learn commands; for example, getting into and out of the box. If we behave as if we are another dog, hide with him and participate in the activity, we are a wonderful funny companion and very stimulating for the animal's brain - there are no limits to creativity!

## 8. Meet my friend!

The dog is a sociable animal that enjoys meeting and sniffing new friends and companions. Walks in the park and visits from friends in the house are ideal occasions for this fast game that activates the dog's intelligence. Simply introduce him to a person and let him smell and explore the person. If he is allowed, the dog can show his affection with a wet lick on face or hands.

## 9. Frisbee throwing

Frisbee throwing is an attractive and motivating game for the dog. He will love running after the disc and catching it.

## 10. Funny dog massage

After so much activity, it is time to relax to regenerate the dog's mind. Why not try a dog massage? With patience and a few tricks (such as finding a quiet place at home or applying gentle pressure on the most sensitive areas such as the neck), the animal's brain can be stimulated by treating it with our hands. A massage on the dog's ears is especially pleasant.

# Thank you

Dear reader,

I am very pleased that you have read this book. My wish for you is that you raise a wonderful puppy and experience many wonderful years with him.

Did the book help you?

Please give me feedback :-)

# Imprint

ISBN: 9798566557090
Imprint: Independently published

Made in the USA
Coppell, TX
09 July 2022

79766295R00100